The Diary of
Ma Yan

The Diary of
Ma Yan

The Daily Life of a
Chinese Schoolgirl

Edited and introduced by
Pierre Haski

Translated from the French by
Lisa Appignanesi

The Diaries were originally translated
from the Mandarin by He Yanping

Virago

A *Virago* Book

First published in Great Britain by Virago Press 2004

Copyright © Éditions Ramsay/Susanna Lea Associates, Paris, 2002

This translation Copyright © Lisa Appignanesi

The moral right of the authors has been asserted

PHOTOGRAPHIC PERMISSIONS
The photos on pages 10, top, 20, 46, 68, 53, 55, 113, 119, 155 are by Wang Zheng.
The photos on the cover and on pages 7, 8, 11, 25, 39, 63, 77, 92, 95, 123, 132,
133, 175, 176, 177, 178, 181, 182 are by Pierre Haski.
The photo of the letter and the diary are by Vincent Angouillant.
The photo of Ma Yan on page 18 was taken by the public photographer in Yuwang.

A CIP catalogue record for this book
is available from the British Library

ISBN 1 84408 076 5

Typeset in Goudy by M Rules
Printed and bound in Great Britain by
Clays Ltd, St Ives plc

Virago Press
An imprint of
Time Warner Book Group UK
Brettenham House
Lancaster Place
London WC2E 7EN

www.virago.co.uk

Acknowledgements

Our sincerest thanks go to translator He Yanping, who has also been engaged in aid work for the children of the Ningxia region; to the photographer, Wang Zheng, who was our guide; to Sarah Neiger, who was instrumental in setting up this adventure; and to all those, both in China and Europe, who have supported Ma Yan and the children of Ningxia.

Contents

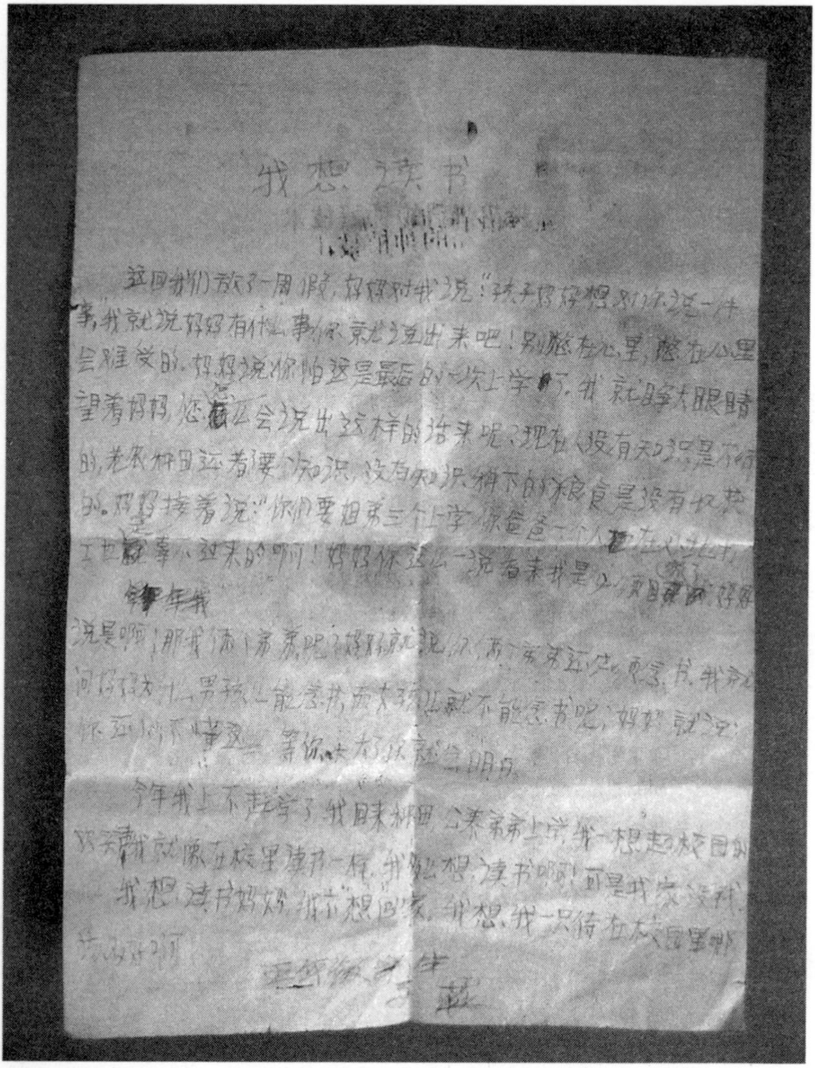

我想读书

这回我们放了一周假，妈妈对我说："孩子妈妈想对你说一件事，我就说妈妈有什么事你就说出来吧！别憋在心里，憋在心里会难受的。妈妈说你怕这是最后的一次上学了。我就睁大眼睛望着妈妈，您怎么会说出这样的话来呢？现在没有知识是不行的，老农种田还需要知识，没有知识，种下的粮食是没有收获的。

Ma Yan's letter, translated opposite.

I Want to Study

We have a week of holidays. Mother takes me aside.

'My child. There's something I have to tell you.'

I answer, 'Mother, if you have something to tell me, do it quickly. Tell me.'

But her words are like a death sentence.

'I'm afraid you may have been to school for the last time.'

My eyes go wide. I look up at her. 'How can you say something like that? These days you can't live without an education. Even a peasant needs knowledge to be sure of good harvests and to farm well.'

Mother insists. 'Your brothers and you make three to be sent to school. Only your father earns money, and that's far away. It's not enough.'

I'm frightened. 'Does that mean I now have to come home to work?'

'Yes.'

'And my two brothers?'

'Your two brothers will carry on with their studies.'

I protest. 'Why can boys study and not girls?'

Her smile is tired. 'You're still little. When you grow up, you'll understand.'

No more money for school this year. I'm back in the house and I till the land in order to pay for my brothers' schooling. When I think of the happy times at school, I can almost imagine myself there. How I want to study! But my family can't afford it.

I want to go to school, Mother. I don't want to work at home. How wonderful it would be if I could stay at school forever!

Ma Yan
2 May 2001

1

How it Happened

Pierre Haski

May 2001. The village of Zhangjiashu thousands of kilometres north-west of Beijing. Our little expedition was getting ready to leave. We were saying goodbye to the local imam who had received us warmly in his home.

In this remote corner of China, children are unaccustomed to seeing strangers. An official had told me that I was the first foreign journalist to come to the region since Edgar Snow – the American reporter who introduced Mao to the Western world in the 1930s in his book *Red Star Over China*. The very sight of us created unusual excitement. But our driver was getting impatient. The road to Yinchuan, the capital of this autonomous region of Ningxia in the north-west of China, would be long and difficult.

At that moment, a village woman wearing the white head-covering of the Chinese Muslims[1] approached a member of our group and urged her towards her house a few metres away. She gave to Sarah Neiger, a friend from Beijing who had organised our long and complicated journey, a letter and three small brown notebooks covered in characters finely drawn in pencil. She insisted, as if her

---

1 China has ten Muslim 'national minorities' totalling over twenty million people out of a total population of 1.3 billion. Among them, the Hui number some nine million and are spread over several Chinese provinces. Ningxia is the only autonomous region attributed to them, even though they form a minority there.

very life depended on it, that Sarah take these with her. A few minutes later we left, carrying this mysterious and apparently precious bundle with us.

When we got back to Beijing, a translation of just a little of what we had been given revealed a startling text, as well as the identity of its author. She was Ma Yan, then a girl of thirteen, in the midst of a crisis. In the letter, addressed in fact to her mother, the very woman who had given us the notebooks, Ma Yan shouts her protest. She has just learned that she won't be able to go back to school. After five consecutive years of drought, her family no longer have the money to pay her school fees.

'I want to study,' Ma Yan exclaims in the headline of the letter written on the back of a seed packet for green beans (see page viii). The letter has been scribbled in anger, as the various tears in the paper show. To pay for the ballpoint pen she used, we later learned that she had deprived herself of food for fifteen days.

The three little brown notebooks that came to us with Ma Yan's letter contained her personal diary. This unique document gives us an intimate sense of the everyday life of a teenager whose life mirrors that of millions of others in the Chinese countryside. Many share her passionate desire for the education which will allow her and her family to escape poverty; many are tortured, like her, by the anxiety that they won't make the grade; many struggle against constant hunger and the bitter, indeed brutal, human relationships which are part of an impoverished peasant life.

The official political line repeats the value of socialism over and over again like a cracked gramophone record. But the state has long abandoned any semblance of responsibility in the Ningxia region. And the Chinese educational system carries on functioning in the interests of the official ideology and seeks to create good Communist citizens in a country which is barely any longer Communist. In remote villages, like that of Zhangjiashu, there is little alternative to the language of Communism. It's there wearing its most attractive face on the state television network, which now puts out the message in stylish MTV-like clips rather than in the agitprop of yesteryear.

This testimony to the extreme hardship of life in remote rural China comes to us in the words of a teenager who, page by page, shows an increasing command both of her writing and of her feelings. Her first days as a schoolgirl in 2000, when she is only thirteen, are the subject of the briefest, most understated notes. Then, before our eyes, Ma Yan gains in stature. The school of this particular life is a tough and fast teacher.

The journal is incomplete. It literally went up in smoke, as we later learned. Ma Yan's father was in the habit of tearing out sheets from his children's notebooks page by page and using them to roll his cigarettes.

The miracle is that we have anything of Ma Yan's diaries at all.

A month after our first visit, we decide to return to Zhangjiashu, this village in the south of Ningxia to meet Ma Yan and her mother. Our first, fleeting encounter had given us a glimpse into a life which is usually secret and barred. We couldn't forewarn anyone of our arrival because means of communication in this part of China have not made the leaps and bounds visible elsewhere.

Zhangjiashu is a little like the end of the world: you don't come upon it by accident. The journey by plane from Beijing to Yinchuan, the modern capital of Ningxia, takes barely an hour. Wang Zheng, a photographer friend, meets us there and we drive for the better of a part of a day on a terrible dirt road. The main road is under construction. The strip crosses the agricultural area around the Yellow River, then snakes through the arid semi-desert out of which sand-coloured villages grow. One of these has been nick-named 'the village of the widows': a number of its male inhabitants, notorious drug traffickers, were condemned to death and executed.

The journey to Zhangjiashu is as much a journey through time as it is through space. The village, whose brick houses roofed with traditional tiles are spread unevenly along the hills, occupies a space far removed from the bubbling modernisation of urban China. During these last two decades, the greatest change to the village has been that it has found a certain kind of peace. The agitation, associated with the large utopian collectives imposed on the countryside by Maoism, has stopped. The land has been returned to the peasants. Electricity has finally arrived.

But the end of the great ideological projects has meant that the village has fallen into a kind of oblivion. Zhangjiashu has been abandoned to its own fate. Its inhabitants were amazed that we had taken under twenty-four hours to get there from Beijing. For them, the capital is light years away.

We arrive to disappointment. Neither Ma Yan nor her mother are in the village. Their house is empty. We finally find the girl's father, Ma Dongshi,[2] a sturdy man who speaks little. He takes us into his small grey-brick house overlooking a valley which is arid as far as the eye can see. He doesn't seem particularly surprised at our presence but he's troubled by the bareness of his home and therefore the simplicity of his welcome.

Ma Yan, he tells us, is at school in Yuwang, the neighbouring commune on which their village depends about twenty kilometres away. When we look surprised, he explains that he and his wife were so troubled by their daughter's letter that they borrowed the money to allow her to finish her school year – seventy yuan.[3] This is a small sum in contemporary China, but it's a fortune here. So, Ma Yan is back at school and is smiling again. Her mother, however, has had to go to work in the north of the province for a few days to harvest

---

2 In China the family name comes before the first name.
3 The basic unit of Chinese currency is the yuan, which is worth approximately 10p. The amount the family borrowed was therefore around £7.

Ma Yan and her parents in front of the family house.

the dreaded *fa cai* (see pages 121–5) so as to be able to pay off the debt.

We go to find Ma Yan in Yuwang, taking the steep road she describes in her diary.

The girl who meets us has short hair and a lot of character. She's simply dressed in a white shirt and red canvas trousers. Around her neck there's a small plastic heart on a chain and she sports two silver-plated hoops in her ears. Lively and intelligent, she beams at us, so very happy to have taken up her school life again. She doesn't hide her joy when she learns that it's because of her we've come.

We walk back with her to the village where an impromptu gathering is taking place in the house of the imam, Hu Dengshuang, an influential man in Zhangjiashu. The head of the village comes along too, as does the secretary of the local Communist Party, the other two important members of the community. Everyone squeezes into

The village of Zhangjiashu.

the imam's living room which is decorated with colour photos of Mecca, and a poster of a tropical beach complete with coconut palms. Cups of tea are passed round.

Then, without any sign of being intimidated Ma Yan begins to speak, recounting her great sadness when she thought she might never be able to return to school. She talks about the gratitude she owes her mother who understood her distress and made the sacrifice of once more going off to do hard labour four hundred kilometres away. She also speaks of the hopes her family has now vested in her, their eldest child. Her sense of duty to her family is linked with defiance. If only she can get far enough with her studies, she'll be the first to escape from the dual burden of a harsh, desert soil and a strictly traditional society. She is fired up by the challenge.

Then, just when everyone is about to leave, a delicate silhouette

8

emerges from the darkness. Bai Juhua,[4] Ma Yan's mother, has unexpectedly come back to the village after her twelve-hour day in the fields. Her features are drawn. A white headscarf covers her long black hair. It takes her only a few seconds to realise what's happening. Her message in a bottle has found a welcoming harbour. We've come back.

Bai Juhua looks at her daughter tenderly. It's clear that the two are very close. Tears start to stream down her weary face. Her emotion is audible in her voice. 'I'm a mother, but my heart was heavy. I knew that I couldn't send my daughter back to school to finish her fifth year. Ma Yan gave me her letter, but I can't read. She insisted, "Read it and you'll know how unhappy I am." I had it read to me and I understood.'

In the imam's living room, everyone is in tears.

Ma Yan's mother, brought low by hard work and poverty, is only thirty-three but she looks twenty years older. She has had no education, she can neither read nor write, but she knows that her daughter's salvation – like that of the rest of her family – depends on her being educated. On several occasions, she had taken Ma Yan from school, once, because the registration fee was 3.5 yuan and she only had three for all her expenses. But at each point, Ma Yan struggled to continue. This girl is stubborn, her father claims proudly.

Bai Juhua tried to get help from the state after she heard on television of the Hope Project which made subsidies available for children of disadvantaged families but her application met with failure. So she went off to harvest *fa cai*. A photograph on her wall at home shows her as pretty and flirtatious, her hair loose and thick, next to other black-and-white pictures of her husband, posing in military uniform in front of a portrait of Mao. Her health and her youth have been sacrificed to the fields.

4 In China, married women keep their maiden names.

Ma Yan at thirteen.

Ma Yan is unusual in this village where most of the girls never have more than three or four years of schooling, barely time enough to learn to read and write, even though schooling in China is meant to go on until the ninth year. Ma Yan is now in her seventh. 'Others stop much sooner,' Ma Yan says sweetly. 'I can only praise my parents.'

Wanting to demonstrate that there are many Ma Yans here, the villagers take us to a small earthen house at a little distance from the others. A reserved teenager, no bigger than Ma Yan, is there, busy helping her parents with domestic tasks. She left school a year ago. When the subject is raised, she bursts out, 'I want to go back to school,' and she rushes off, crying. Her parents don't speak, they stare at the ground. As poor as Ma Yan's parents, they have even fewer resources and ways of coping.

Bai Juhua found comfort in the support of Ma Yan's teachers. At Yuwang, a teacher told her: 'Your daughter is one of our best students. She really mustn't stop. If you take her out of school, you're

The barren landscape and archaic farming methods of the region.

ruining her future.' The imam, who had Ma Yan as a pupil in her first two years at the village primary, concurred. 'She's very bright, quick, and a good worker. She could go as far as university.'

University! Some of the daughters of Yuwang's most prominent families have got there, but for a peasant girl it's an all but impossible dream.

We spend the night at the imam's house. At four-thirty, his wife is already up preparing a copious breakfast: mutton, noodle soup, a selection of vegetables, steamed bread. Poverty does not lessen the villagers' sense of hospitality. We've barely finished eating when Ma Yan comes to find us. Her mother, too, has prepared breakfast and it's impossible to refuse her invitation. This breakfast turns out to be just as large as the first. Then, once more, someone comes to fetch us. The village head wants to invite us to breakfast.

We take Ma Yan to her school in Yuwang. She walks through the doors with pride and confidence: our promised help means she is certain to be able to carry on with her studies for at least another term, if not longer.

This story could well have stopped there. But a few months later, in March 2002, we went back to Ningxia with a larger aim: we wanted to help more children continue their education. An article on Ma Yan had been published in the Paris newspaper *Libération* on 11 January. It seemed that a great many readers were prepared to help Ma Yan with her schooling. Translated into Italian, the article met with similar enthusiasm from readers in Italy.

During our last visit to Zhangjiashu, a Chinese friend from the regional capital who had accompanied us had mocked our desire to help Ma Yan. Adversity and the weight of tradition would finish by bringing the girl down, as they had done others in the village, he told us.

'A family as poor as hers can't afford to pay for their daughter's education. She'll be engaged at sixteen, because her family needs the money her marriage will bring in to pay for their two younger sons' marriages. The boys will take precedence.' (In China, it's the husband who pays the equivalent of a dowry to the family for his future bride.) 'Ma Yan is intelligent, but she can't escape that fate. It's her unalterable destiny.'

But Ma Yan's mother denied this categorically. 'I'll fight to my last breath so that my daughter doesn't have the same life as I had. When Ma Yan becomes a mother, she'll understand what an effort I made for her.'

If she could read her daughter's diary, she would know that Ma Yan already recognises her enormous debt. She understands the price her mother has paid to send her to school and that she's indebted to what she calls her 'mother's hands'.

Here is a woman of no education, married against her will, whose life until now has been one long run of trials, and yet it is she who has inculcated in her daughter the fundamental value of effort and perseverance. Through her hard work, she has maintained a family on the razor's edge of subsistence. Then, by some extraordinary intuition, she handed us her daughter's diaries and gave her a more certain future. Bai Juhua and Ma Yan are both heroines of this story.

When mother and daughter hug each other that night at the imam's house, there's more at stake than just strong emotion. The energy that flows between them is that of two women prepared to confront and challenge fate.

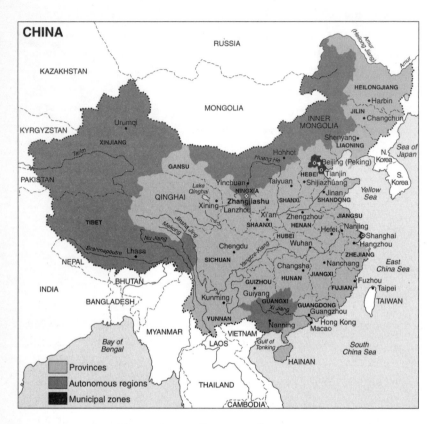

Map of China showing Zhangjiashu⊗, Ma Yan's village.

The Diary

The diaries of Ma Yan are divided into two parts. The first period runs from 2 September to 28 December 2000; the second from 3 July to 13 December 2001. The breaks are due to the lost notebooks. The dates used here are those of the official Chinese calendar which dictates the school year. Official China and urban China follow the Gregorian calendar, but Chinese tradition, like rural life, still obeys a lunar cycle.

Ma Yan started school at eight, one year after most other pupils. Until then she helped her mother with domestic chores and in the fields. Her first four school years were spent at primary school in Zhangjiashu. For her fifth year she went to the Hui primary school in Yuwang, twenty kilometres away from home. At the time the diary starts, she's boarding. In order to buy her school books and to get used to the place, she arrived a week before the start of term.

Ma Yan is thirteen at her first entry, in her last year of primary school. Her diary stops when she is in the first year of senior school and fourteen years old.

The diaries have been annotated and a commentary included in order to clarify aspects of her daily life.

The sections at the back of the book place the diary within the context of China and follow up the story of Ma Yan. They also include readers' letters and an account of how an association was formed to sponsor Chinese children's schooling.

We are perhaps only at the beginning of an exceptional human adventure . . .

PART ONE

Ma Yan in the studio of the public photographer
in Yuwang. The backdrop depicts a beach,
of which there are none in Ningxia!

Saturday 2 September (2000).
It's not very grey.

Just like every morning, I wash my face then brush my teeth. Soon the bell that marks the beginning of classes rings. A teacher arrives. He's wearing a blue jacket and black trousers and he has black leather shoes. He explains what he expects of us. I think he's our Chinese teacher.

A second teacher comes in. He tells us never to take things that belong to others and to think very carefully about what we say. Then he starts the lesson and gives us exercises to do. We do the work he's asked of us until class is over.

We go off to eat. Bai Xiaohua, in class three of the fifth year, brings in a pail full of water. We wash our faces and hands and then clean the dormitory. Bai Xiaohua sprinkles water on the floor. Yang Haiyan shakes out the beds. Ma[5] Yuehua and I sweep the floor. Ma Juan has gone out, I don't know where, instead of helping us. Having done the cleaning we sit down to rest for a bit, until the bell rings again.

5 The second name, Ma, is a very common one among the Hui Muslims in China.

This morning, while I was busy working in class, my father and mother came to visit. They came to Yuwang for the fair.[6] Before going back to it, they said to me: 'You must work hard in order to get into the high school for girls.' Then they went.

6 Ma Yan's village of Zhangjiashu is part of the commune of Yuwang, where her school is located. This is also a major market town.

Ma Yan's father and mother are quite different from one another. Very tall, with a pudding-basin haircut and taci-turn, inhibited manner, Ma Dongji comes from a very poor family. His father was the son of a beggar who had been sold to a landowner in Zhangjiashu in the 1930s. Bai Juhua, Ma Yan's mother, comes from a more comfortably off family who live in a village thirty-five kilometres away. She is chatty and impulsive, with a ready smile and long hair hidden behind her white scarf.

Like many rural marriages even today, their union was arranged, in this case by an aunt in Zhangjiashu. She was sixteen, he was twenty-three. 'Ma Dongji was just back from the army. He was tall and handsome. But I didn't want him. My mother said, "If he's been through the army, that means the Communists like him. I do, too. Why don't you?"' Bai Juhua tells us.

Deprived of schooling and destined for an early mar-riage, Bai Juhua bent to the family will. It was almost impossible for her to do otherwise at that time. She made the long journey to her in-laws' house on a tractor and from then on was effectively theirs to rule.

Ma Dongji and Bai Juhua have three children: Ma Yan, the eldest, thirteen in the year 2000, and two boys, Ma Yichao, eleven, and Ma Yiting, nine, that year.

Despite the population politics – a single child per family – championed for some two decades, rural parents are allowed to have two children, and three if the first is a girl.

Monday 4 September.
Light rain.

This afternoon, a teacher showed us some gymnastics. If we can't do them, we have to get out of line and sing or dance. Then we have to start again, until we've managed to get through all the exercises. A few comrades, both boys and girls, finally managed it all and the teacher congratulated them: 'Those who've succeeded can go back to class.'

Finally we all got through and went back to our classrooms.

Tuesday 5 September.
Fine weather.

This afternoon, the music teacher, a twenty-year-old woman with a plait over a metre long, taught us the 'Song of the Long March'. She is our only woman teacher. First, she sings with us a few times, then she lets us sing in chorus. Then she chooses one of us to sing alone, and another to dance in accompaniment. Everyone gets a turn, row by row. We've only reached the third row when the bell rings.

Wednesday 6 September.
A grey day.

This afternoon, our Chinese teacher gave us an exercise to copy into our notebook. Two boys fought over a pencil,[7] as often happens. Before we even realised what had happened, the teacher had smacked them.[8] I couldn't help but be secretly pleased: these two are the nastiest boys in class.

---

7 Each pupil has to bring his own materials to school. Nothing is supplied.
8 Corporal punishment is much used in this school, as in many other rural establishments, though technically it's forbidden. Ma Yan explained to us that this teacher hits the pupils very hard across the neck. Others use a ruler or a pointer.

Thursday 7 September.
Fine weather.

This morning, we had Chinese. The teacher wrote a few questions on the blackboard and asked us to answer them. It's a matter of summarising a text. He explained to us that if we don't know all the words, we can look them up in a dictionary.

I borrowed one from a friend because my father couldn't buy one for me.[9] I was so busy consulting it that I forgot to write down the rest of the questions which were then erased.

I asked my aunt, Ma Shiping, to lend me her notebook so that I could copy them out, but she refused. She thinks this is an exam, and she doesn't want me to come first.

It's a little thing, but it makes me realise that I can count on no one.

9 The school has no library and no teaching materials to aid the pupils.

Ma Yan's family is an extensive one. Apart from her paternal grandparents, the village of Zhangjiashu contains the families of her father's four brothers, whom Ma Jan designates according to their chronological age: 'first uncle, second uncle' and so on. Thus her father, who is the second youngest of the brothers, would be referred to as uncle number four.

Ma Shiping, whom Ma Yan describes as her 'aunt', is in fact her cousin at second remove. She is her mother's cousin and is two years older than her. Their stormy relations are due to reciprocal admiration and jealousy. Despite her strong personality and good grades Ma Shiping had to finish school at the end of that year, her last of primary school. Seventh of ten children, the girl had to devote herself to domestic and farm work, until she was married.

This morning during the class, the Chinese teacher taught us that in life a man has to act according to two principles: his values and his dignity. This will ensure the respect of others.

At the end of class, he warned us to be careful on the road on our way home. Those who have money can get a lift on a tractor for one yuan. The rest of us have to walk. But we mustn't dawdle.

The road to school is long and dangerous.

At Friday lunchtime, which marks the end of the school week, Ma Yan sets off on the twenty-kilometre walk to her village. In snow, rain or blistering sun, Ma Yan and her brother, Ma Yichao, who is in the same class as her, trudge along a dusty road which snakes through the hilly countryside. The route is made up of a long monotonous walk through ploughed fields, a dangerous stretch bordered by a ravine, steep climbs and descents, then a gap between yawning cliffs. It takes four hours if you walk quickly, five if you slow down.

This stark variety of landscapes offers little shelter along the way in bad weather because few people live here. Often by the time the children arrive home, they are soaked through or frozen by glacial winds, their feet swollen. Even in snow or mud, Ma Yan wears the canvas shoes her mother has made and these soak up water quickly.

The road home can also present the children with unpleasant encounters (see page 78). According to Ma Yan, these thieves are often adolescents from other villages. Once, they were held up by older teenagers who refused to let them pass unless they gave them bread, money and their schoolbags. The children managed to escape by each running off in a different direction. Another time, Ma Yan's youngest brother was hit and had to give up his school things, his pencils and his rubber.

Saturday 9 September.
A fine day.

This morning, while we were watching a soap opera,[10] my little brothers who were playing outside, started to shout, 'Our grandmother has arrived!'

My mother beamed. I went to join my brothers outside. We skipped rope and kicked a sandbag around. My grandmother and my mother stayed in the house alone. I don't know what they were talking about, but they laughed in a strange way.

10 Two television channels are available in the village: CCTV, the national channel, and also a regional channel. The family's black-and-white television was bought as a bargain for 400 yuan (£40) when Ma Yan's parents had come back from a stint of work outside the village.

Ma Yan's mother's family lives thirty-five kilometres away in a mountain village to the north of Yuwang. The family is much 'richer' than that of her father. They own 100 mu of land (approximately one-fifteenth of a hectare or one-sixth of an acre), having done well out of the state redistribution in the 1980s (see page 129).

'We had more to eat in the family house,' Bai Juhua tells us. 'When I saw my husband's father's house, small and dark and neglected, I wondered how a veteran of the Korean War could live so badly. I was surprised that his life was so hard.'

She also remembers the hostility of the villagers, who had only contempt for her in-laws. 'Useless people,' they said to me. 'How else to explain the fact that they can't find work even though they've been through the army. I was advised to divorce and leave.' She stayed and became the pillar of her family.

Ma Yan's maternal grandparents criticise the paternal branch a great deal and rarely come to visit their daughter at home. 'They also give us very few presents,' Ma Yan notes. 'Sometimes a few apples or pears or peaches.'

The rivalry between the two families is one of Ma Yan's primary motives for wanting to study. She wants her mother's family to stop being contemptuous of her father. She wants to prove that his offspring can succeed.

Sunday 10 September.
It's windy.

This morning, my grandmother and my parents went to the fair in Yuwang while I was still asleep. My little brothers turned everything upside down and I was in a rage. But there's nothing to be done.

The family house.

Ma Yan's family's most important asset is the little brick house that they've built for themselves. It consists of a single large room, of which half is taken up by the *kang*, the vast traditional bed, made of cement and heated from beneath, on which the whole family eats, sleeps and lives.

There are few ornaments. On the whitewashed walls, pride of place is given to Ma Yan and her brother's end-of-year diplomas, precious objects in this family of illiterates. On top of a basic chest, two frames display family photos. The only luxury in the house is the black-and-white television set. An adjacent space serves as a kitchen and storeroom. In front of the house, there's a small kitchen garden and a fenced space for animals: chickens, a donkey, and a few sheep.

Monday 11 September.
A fine day.

This afternoon, my aunt Ma Shiping came to fetch my brother, Ma Yichao, and me for the walk back to school.

Before letting us go, Mother stopped us to say: 'You need to work hard. Even if I have to wear myself out, I'll pay for your studies but on the condition that your grades are good.'

My mother's words tug at my heart. I understand that everything she does is for us. I understand that we're her only hope. Nothing else counts, but us.

I have to study hard to make a contribution to my country and my people one day. That's my goal. That's my hope.

Yuwang is part of the southern tip of Ningxia, organised around the Xi Hai Gu triangle (a compound of the districts of Xiji, Haichuan and Guyuan), one of the poorest parts of China.

Xi Hai Gu is known as the region of thirst. Drought is now chronic and has led the government to declare the area uninhabitable. None the less, some three million people, half the population of the province, still live in this part of the region. Most of them are Hui, but some are also members of the dominant Han ethnicity.[11] They live here despite the fact that daily life is a constant struggle for survival. The number of children is one of the factors which enforces rural poverty, since the families divide the land between their sons. In villages where the Han ethnic minority is dominant, the number of children is reduced and the parcels of land are therefore greater. A Han official to whom we talked about the poverty of the Hui villages, retorted: 'All they have to do is respect family planning rules and things would immediately be better for them . . .'

The average annual income of the inhabitants of Ma Yan's village is around 400 yuan, a miserable sum compared to the Chinese average of 6,000 yuan, let alone the Shanghai average of 33,000 yuan. Even the crumbs of the great Chinese economic expansion have failed to reach this far. This Far West is simply forgotten by the rich and distant bureaucrats of central power: too small, too far away, too docile. It's really just like in the old days of the fallen Chinese empires.

11 The Hans get their name from the dynasty which ruled China soon after the creation of a unified empire some 2,200 years ago.

Tuesday 12 September.
Lovely weather.

This afternoon I went out with a couple of classmates to run some errands. They're rich. They're always chomping away at one goodie or another. I watch them, but I can't afford to buy anything. Even chewing gum costs over ten fen.[12] That's far more than I can manage.

I suddenly realise why Mother doesn't get medical help.[13] It's so that we can carry on going to school. School costs tens of yuan all at once. Where does this money come from? It comes from the sweat and hard labour of my parents. Father and Mother are ready to sacrifice everything so that we can go to school. I must work really hard in order to go to university later. Then I'll get a good job and Mother and Father will at last have a happy life.

12 A yuan is made up of 100 fen; 10 fen equals around 1p.
13 Ma Yan's mother has terrible stomach pains and spits blood.

Those who Ma Yan calls 'rich' are mostly children from the commune of Yuwang rather than those who come from the surrounding villages. Their parents are civil servants or business people, professions which guarantee a certain revenue and a social status above that of peasant. Ma Yan's 'rich' are those who have a real wardrobe, whereas she hasn't a single change of clothes; those who have pocket money whereas she can't even pay for vegetables to go with the rice she eats in the school dormitory.

Children quickly register such differences, just as Ma Yan and her friends would have been aware that compared to urban Chinese, both groups are at the bottom of the social scale.

Wednesday 13 September.
A lovely day.

Today, after school, my brother Yichao and I went to find our mother. She was at the doctor's on Yuwang's main street. I wanted to leave straight after seeing her in order to get back to school and work. I just needed to stop and buy some shampoo. But Mother wouldn't let us go. She promised that when she was finished with the doctor, she would buy us something to eat.

All three of us went to the market. Mother bought us some food for dinner, but nothing for herself, so we had to eat it alone. I could clearly see that she was hungry and thirsty.

If she's depriving herself like this, it's so that we can live and work.

I have to do well and take the competitive university entrance exam, then find work so that Mother can eat until she's completely full and leads a better life.

In fact, Ma Yan's mother has confided her ill-health to a practitioner from the coastal province of Fujian. He's an acupuncturist who works on a stool on the pavement. She paid fifty yuan for six sessions which were intended to ease her terrible stomach pains. But the man disappeared after the third session and was never seen again in Yuwang.

The proliferation of charlatans of this type is due to the inaccessibility of health care to the poor. Both medical care and medicine now have to be paid for in China. In the Maoist era, the system of 'barefoot doctors' guaranteed everyone free basic health care.

According to the Ministry of Health, 36 per cent of peasants requiring treatment don't go to a doctor, while 61 per cent leave hospital before the end of treatment because of a lack of finances. At the hospital in Yinchuan where we eventually took Bai Juhua to have her problem seen to, the consultation and treatment for what turned out to be an ulcer cost 300 yuan.

In 2002, the government announced a plan which would guarantee basic health cover for all Chinese by 2010, but the financing of this ambitious project is still open to question.

'The large rural Chinese population shouldn't be deprived of basic medical care because of a lack of money. Innovative ideas for finding funds and robust political will are necessary to end this intolerable suffering.' This was the view of Hong Kong's *South China Morning Post* on 12 June 2002.

Thursday 14 September.
Good weather.

During the maths class this morning, the teacher asked me to dis-tribute the exercise books and to collect the simultaneous workbooks.[14] There were thirty-seven in all. None can be over-looked.

I don't want to be head of maths.[15] But I can't refuse. I can't dis-appoint the teacher. I have to carry on doing everything I'm asked so that I can bring home the ultimate victory.[16]

Friday 15 September.
Good weather.

At eleven in the morning, after the last class of the day, we left school and went home for the weekend. The classes stop at the end of the morning to give us time to get back to our villages. There are seven of us, boys and girls. Two friends, Ma Yuehua and Ma Juan, take a tractor that costs one yuan. The rest of us, including my brother and my aunt, Ma Shiping, walk.

I'm always afraid on this road. The ravines on either side are very deep, the mountains dangerously steep. Sometimes thieves stop us and demand money.

14 In the printed 'simultaneous' workbooks – usually for maths problems or for Chinese writing and grammar – the pupil has to fill in the blanks. They work in parallel with a course book.
15 There is a head student for each subject who liaises between teacher and pupils and enforces discipline.
16 Like all Chinese children, Ma Yan is full of slogans learned by rote in the Young Pioneers, the youth movement of the Communist Party. Paradoxically, these Maoist clichés live on in education, whereas they have lost their meaning in a society which has moved further and further away from basic Communist ideology.

Saturday 16 September.
A nice day.

This morning Mother went to the market in Yuwang. She was no sooner back in the house than she started shouting at my brothers and me. Then she began to get dinner ready: rice and salted cabbage.[17] When we'd finished eating she went into her room and cried and cried.

I know why she's in tears. She's ill and she's the only one working in the fields, right now. We're in the midst of harvest and on top of that, Mother has to look after the little ox she's bought to help till the land.[18] Father has gone to find work in Hohhot in Inner Mongolia.

If someone as brave as my mother cries when she's ill, how will the rest of us ever manage?

17 In Ma Yan's family, meat is a rare luxury. Several months can go by, even a year, without its being served.
18 The ox, bought with the parents' hard-earned cash, has started to lose its hair while working outside the village. 'I cried. He was dying, I was going to lose everything,' Bai Juhua explained. Finally she was able to sell it, but at a loss.

Since the land doesn't produce enough to feed his family, Ma Yan's father, like tens of millions of other Chinese peasants, tries to find work elsewhere. Several times a year he goes off to Yinchuan, the capital of Ningxia, or to Hohhot in Inner Mongolia, Gansu or Shaanxi, two other neighbouring provinces, to find work on construction sites in order to supplement his other work on the land.

'You can earn up to 400 or 500 yuan, but often enough, the bosses don't pay up,' he complains.

Ma Dongji is not suited to making his way in a jungle where the predators are always on the watch for peasants like him. He would far rather hire out his labour to another local farmer at harvest time.

Ma Yan's father, Ma Dongji.

Sunday 17 September.
A grey day.

This afternoon my aunt, my brother and I left to go back to school in Yuwang. When we arrived, the door of the dormitory wasn't open yet. We waited for quite a while before the porter turned up.

As soon as we were allowed in, Ma Shiping started to write in her diary. 'Will you be finished soon?' I asked her. 'No,' she answered. 'We can't all be as quick and clever as you.'

She must have thought I was making fun of her.

I wonder why everyone is so displeased with me.

Monday 18 September.
A windy day.

This afternoon, my little brother Ma Yichao, who is in the same class as me, didn't line up properly for the gym class. The head of the class and the head of the gym rushed to give him a beating. The teacher permitted it.

Deep down, I'm in a rage. But what can I do? These two heads are the nastiest boys in the class.

If I study very hard and make daily progress, I'll go to university and become a policewoman.[19] And if these boys bend the law even a tiny little bit, I won't fail to have them punished.

Tuesday 19 September.
Good weather.

This afternoon we had a music lesson. Ma Shengliang, Ma Xiaoping and my brother, Ma Yichao, forgot their books.

19 Ma Yan admits that she's only ever seen a policeman on the television, since there are none in her village. But with a father and a grandfather who served in the army, her desire for order and to serve the community is not surprising.

The teacher told them off. 'You're really stupid. You come here to work and you don't even bring your books!'

Then she tells the first two to leave the class and go and stand outside in the sun without moving. Only then does she begin our lesson.

Wednesday 20 September.
A grey day.

This afternoon, the natural sciences teacher, Chen, gives us a lesson on nature. Ma Fulong talks and acts stupid at the back of the room.

The teacher pulls him up by the collar and tells him to sit up straight. Some of my friends say the teacher is very nasty; others that he was right to discipline the pupils since one shouldn't talk in class.

I think the teacher is right, because on this road to our future life, we have to take the right track and not wander off on a mistaken one.

Thursday 21 September.
A fine day.

This afternoon, after school, the class head orders us to go and get our meal in the kitchen. We had rice but no vegetables. I wanted to borrow some from my aunt, Ma Shiping, but she poured her entire ration of potatoes into her rice bowl and said there was no more.

'It doesn't matter,' I said and asked my friend, Ma Yuehua, for some vegetables. She grumbled a bit but she's nicer than my aunt and gave me a little.

I understand that you can't depend on relatives. If someone outside the family borrows something from you, then she'll remember you've done her a good turn. But if it's a member of the family, she won't want to lend you anything, even if you're unhappy. It's just not her problem.

I've at last cracked the nature of human relations. Everyone pays back their debts to others.

Apart from the registration fee and the cost of books (almost 200 yuan per term), boarders have to provide their own rice. This doubles the termly expenditure. Twice a year, at the beginning of term, schoolchildren have to bring a sack of 25 kilos of rice to school. This lunch rice is cooked in large cauldrons by women who do the cooking for the whole school in one of the school buildings.

Each pupil gets a bowl of rice from them that he goes back to his dormitory to eat. If they want an extra spoonful of vegetables, usually potatoes, they have to pay an additional ten fen. There's never any meat. There are no other meals, neither breakfast nor dinner.

Ma Yan eats nothing in the morning and has to make do with her lunchtime bowl of rice, since she has no money for vegetables. She eats a bit of steamed roll at dinner, which her mother has made and which she keeps in a box.

If they have any money, pupils can go out into Yuwang and buy food from stalls in the streets. But Ma Yan only gets one yuan a week for pocket money. She prefers to buy a pencil or a notebook with that. Only when she goes home at the weekends can Ma Yan hope to satisfy her hunger.

Friday 22 September.
A fine day.

We came home from school this afternoon after the end of classes. After dinner, Mother asked us to go to the buckwheat fields to bring back the bales that had already been cut. I couldn't really walk any further, but Mother forced us to go. She had already harvested so much of the grain herself, how could we refuse her, especially since Father is still away working in Inner Mongolia.

It's in order to feed and clothe us that Mother works so hard. If not, she wouldn't have to harvest buckwheat.[20] It's right that she asks us and equally right that we help. Otherwise how would we merit all the trouble she takes over us? She wears herself out so that we can have a different future from hers. She exhausts herself to provide food for us when there's nothing left, and then she exhausts herself all over again, without getting anything out of life for herself. She doesn't want us to live the way she does. That's why we have to study. We'll be happy. Unlike her.

---

20 Buckwheat is planted between two wheat harvests because it takes only two months to ripen.

Children take part in all the farming work (see page 112) when they're not at school. They help in the harvesting of cereals, feed the animals, fetch water from the wells. The Ma family, like most of the poor peasants in the region, depend on human labour, sometimes with the help of a donkey or a small ox. They have almost no access to fertilisers or pesticides. Only 'the rich' have a tractor, which costs about 6,000 yuan. Their owners have usually earned the money for it by working in town or in the *fa cai* trade.

Harvesting is done with a scythe. The yield shows that seven kilos of seed produces fifty kilos of grain per mu in a good year, and half that amount in a bad year. Ningxia has a continental climate with severe and long winters which last from October onwards. There's snow and frost. In summer, it's very hot with temperatures reaching 40 degrees centigrade. It rains mostly in spring and autumn.

'In years when there's no rain,' Ma Yan's father explains, 'there's an expectation that at least you'll get back what you planted so that you can start again.'

Ma Yan's family has eight mu of land. Two of these are occupied by the house, which means that only six mu are available for agriculture – an area which isn't nearly large enough to provide for a family.

This morning I was in the middle of doing homework when Mother interrupted me.

'Come, we're going to beat the grain.'[21]

My big sister, Ma Yimei, my little sister, Ma Yifang,[22] my two brothers, my mother and I, all work together on the stretch of land in front of our house.

Suddenly the son of Yang Dangqi arrives in his tractor which is full of buckwheat and he dumps his harvest in front of our house. Mother asks him to leave, but he just sneers. She asks a second time, and he still does nothing. She's very angry and she starts calling him names.

In my heart of hearts, I think he's a scoundrel. He takes other people's places on the beating stretch, pretending it's first come, first served. And it's useless for us to protest.

In these times, even beggars need degrees. Nothing works for you if you don't study. In the big cities, even going to the toilet requires being able to read.

---

21 The bundles of buckwheat are placed on a flat surface and beaten with a large stone in order to husk the grain.

22 In fact, these are cousins.

Sunday 24 September.
A nice day.

This afternoon on the way to school, we meet a man pulling an ox. He's accompanied by a second man who holds his jacket in his hand. They tell us about their childhood.

When they went to school, shepherds would stop them on their way and demand bread. They ask us if there are still people who block the road and don't let you pass. 'Less than before,' we say. 'You're lucky,' they say.

Agricultural methods have remained traditional.

Monday 25 September.
A grey day.

At noon, in the history lesson, the teacher asks us several questions. I don't know any of the answers. Luckily, he hasn't chosen me. He's singled out my younger brother and two other students, who don't know the answers either. Only my aunt, Ma Shiping, tall and proud, with her long plait, answered correctly. The teacher complimented her. I admire her. She's so clever.

Tuesday 26 September.
A grey day.

A music lesson this afternoon. After the class, the teacher organises games for us. We play blind man's buff and whoever is caught has to sing and dance. The first group creates a song-and-dance number and then the second group.

'Which of the two is better?' asks the music teacher.

Everyone agrees it was the second group who were remarkable.

I have to take note of these girls and do well in all my classes, including music.

Wednesday 27 September.
A fair day.

This afternoon we went back to the dormitory[23] after our classes. I saw that Ma Yuehua was writing something. The head of the dormitory, Ma Jing, asked her to clean the floor.

'I'll do it when I've finished my work,' she answered without lifting her nose from her book. The head of the dorm wouldn't

---

23 Most of the children in the school are boarders. The dormitories are rooms which have space only for beds, ten per room for the children in the last year of primary; sixteen per room for the older ones.

take no for an answer. She insisted that Ma Yuehua clean up instantly. If she doesn't, she'll report her to the teacher.

Ma Yuehua weeps her rage.

Thursday 28 September.
A grey day.

This afternoon, my aunt, Ma Shiping, Li Qing and I went to Yuwang to buy bread. In the first bakery we came to, the bread was very small, so we didn't buy any. We found a second bakery and decided to go in. I said: 'I will have a piece of bread and a twisty doughnut.'

The assistant handed them to me. When I was leaving the bakery, he made a joke behind my back.

Is it because we're country girls or because I pronounced the word 'bread' badly? I'll never know.

Peasants in the city are objects of derision. This is especially true in metropolises like Shanghai or Beijing but it is also true in provincial centres like Yuwang, where the inhabitants treat the peasants in the same way that they themselves are treated elsewhere.

You quickly learn how to spot a migrant from the country. His skin has a coppery tone. His manner is uncertain. On top of that, there's the lack of respect which city people show him. They've forgotten that they too have roots in the country.

Regional accents also help to betray the origin of a person, who becomes the object of contempt once his or her accent is singled out as not 'noble' enough.

Ma Yan in the street outside her dilapidated secondary school.

Friday 29 September.
Light rain.

At lunchtime when we leave for home after classes, it's very cold. It's raining, too. The other girls in my dorm are getting lifts home on a tractor. There's only my brother and me and one other pupil who are walking.

We come to a spot where the water has washed away the strip of road and we can't get through. My brother puts his foot on a rock and leaps across, making it to another rock. He pulls me by the hand and I get across too. In turn I give my hand to the other girl and pull her across to our side. We finally manage to get up the slope and are out of danger.

Saturday 30 September.
A grey day

This morning, just after I had eaten a bowl of yellow rice for breakfast, I sat down to read 'Voyage to the West'[24] which a school friend lent me. Suddenly I heard two tractors coming along the road towards our house.

People say that these two tractors will build up the track. This is really good news. Once this work is done, no one will any longer be able to say that we live 'on the island of Taiwan'.[25]

---

24 By Xiyouji, this is one of the great Chinese classics, alongside *The Dream of the Red Pavilion*, *On the Banks of the River* and *The Book of the Three Kingdoms*. Written in the fifteenth century, *Voyage to the West* recounts the adventures of a monk and a monkey who travel towards India in search of the canons of Buddhism.

25 The villagers joked that with the subsidence of the slope, the family's house, located on a small hill, was moving further and further away – just like the island of Taiwan was distancing itself more and more from Mother China.

Sunday 1 October.
A fine day.

This morning, on the day of the national holiday,[26] the weather is particularly beautiful. My maternal grandmother who lives in a village to the north of Yuwang is ill and my mother decides to go and see her. But an hour later, she's changed her mind and no longer wants to go.

I ask her: 'Why don't you want to go and see Grandmother?'

'I'll go tomorrow when I have to go to the market in Yuwang,' she says.

I ask again, 'Why, why don't you go today?'

'I'll go when I've done the housework.'

'Don't worry about it,' I say to reassure her. 'I can do it. I'm big enough. Really.'

Mother smiles. 'You really are grown-up!'

She finally did go to see Grandmother, on a bicycle she borrowed from her aunt, and with my youngest brother riding behind.

26 The holiday celebrates the declaration of the People's Republic of China by Mao Zedong on 1 October 1949.

Monday 2 October.
A fine day.

This morning the men are repairing the road with their tractors. They don't know where to get earth to shore it up and the road subsides more and more.

A lot of people are watching from the distance of the hill and laughing. I don't know why they're laughing.

My cousin hears them and explains. 'They're making fun. They're saying that when this road is finally finished, you'll definitely be living in Taiwan.'

When she hears this, Mother is in a rage. She asks the workers to remove the earth from in front of our door, in order to create a wide access road for us.

'Clear this earth away so that we can live!' she protests.

Once the earth has been used to bank up the track, some people start to mock again: 'This is a really good road. What dreams Ma Dongji must have had.'[27]

Really, people come out with the most ridiculous things these days!

---

27 The allusion is to Ma Yan's father who must have had a dream like the one in the legend in which the peasant dreams that the mountain in front of his house is flattened.

Tuesday 3 October.
A fine day.

Very early this morning, Mother wakes my brother Ma Yichao, so that he can help her get the donkey ready for work. Mother walks in front, while my brother controls the donkey from behind. I can see all the wrinkles on my mother's face.

She's ageing, and all because she wants to fill our stomachs and assure our future.

Ma Yan and her mother on the evening when
we returned to the village.

Deprived of education herself, Ma Yan's mother has above all instilled in her daughter the desire to learn. In a soft voice and without a trace of self-pity she says, 'I only did a year of school. I wasn't able to learn anything, except to sing and dance. Then my mother brought me home to stay. That's why I so much want Ma Yan to study. If not, her future will be bleak. If she studies, she'll get a good job. People will look up to her, rather than looking down.'

Bai Juhua explains to us that village tradition still insists that girls without education should submit to arranged marriages. And that means most of the girls of the village.

'For these girls, to find their own husband is to lose face.'

Losing face, one quickly learns in China, is worse than anything else. You can die of it.

Ma Yan's mother tells us the story of a young couple who met while working away from home on the *fa cai* fields. They liked each other. But the girl's mother preferred a young man back home and told her, 'You can't afford to make light of losing face.' She forced her to marry a boy who 'squinted', but whose family paid them 1,200 yuan worth of jewels. Such is country life.

For all these reasons, Bai Juhua tells her daughter that she has to do well at school, even better than her brothers. She wasn't able to help her children with their school work but when they were at the primary school in the village, every day she would ask them to write out what they had learned on the hard clay soil in front of the house.

'Neither her father nor I could understand what Ma Yan was studying,' she adds with a sad expression.

Wednesday 4 October.
A fine day.

We're still home on holiday and I'm in the process of doing my home-work. My aunt, Ma Shiping, who's in the same class as I am, comes over to play. We play hide and seek with my brothers. I tell Ma Shiping that if she can find me, I'll explain one of the maths problems to her. She replies that she knows all her maths by heart and goes off.

I think to myself that, deep down, the only person I can count on is myself.

Thursday 5 October.
A fine day.

This morning Mother wants to winnow the rice in order to remove the husks. When she opens up the rice bags, she finds mice in them. She flies into a rage and tells us off in the severest way.

I was supposed to make sure the door to the storeroom was always closed and I forgot. The mice got in. And that's why Mother is so angry.

Entire families, even the very young, work in the fields.

55

Friday 6 October.
A fine day.

This afternoon, my mother, my aunt Ma Shiping and my sisters[28] were discussing things at home. After that, my aunt, who is not much older than I am, asked me to turn on the tape recorder so we could dance. I danced with my little sister. At first, no one else danced. But by the end everyone was twirling and their faces grew red with excitement. This was my happiest day.

Saturday 7 October.
A grey day.

This afternoon, after doing my other work, I started to do my home-work. I heard my little brother, Ma Yichao, crying. He's stretched out on the bed. I ask him why he's crying. He says he didn't manage to do the exercises in his workbook. He still has to fill in the blank spaces. I help him do it.

After a little while, I tell him I need to do my own work now, and he must finish his on his own. If I don't finish it today, the teacher will reprimand me and hit me.

Mother walks by. 'You're really very silly.' She launches an attack on me.

I'm astonished. Why has she told me off like that? Have I said something really stupid? I feel terribly sad. Nothing is too much effort where her son is concerned, but I have to make do best I can.

I feel so alone. There's no one to talk to.

---

28 Again Ma Yan must be referring to her cousins.

Despite Mao's saying that 'Women are half of heaven', fifty years of Communism have done little to institute equality between the sexes. This is particularly true in remote regions like the villages of Ningxia. But even in the cities, equality remains a dream. Bai Juhua, Ma Yan's mother, is well aware of it: if her daughter's teachers hadn't insisted, Ma Yan would have left school a long time ago, while her brothers would carry on with their studies.

The logic is inarguable. Once a girl gets married, she leaves her own family for that of her husband's. All the investment made in her education is lost to her original family.

Hu Dengshuang, the imam of Zhangjiashu, recognises that in the villages boys are favoured. 'Women are seen as labourers. Some never go to school at all. I try and tell people to leave their girls at school as long as possible. I believe in equality. But when a family has run out of money, it's girls who suffer first.'

Chinese families prefer to have a boy rather than a girl. One of Ma Yan's aunts has even had seven daughters, in complete violation of the family planning laws (see page 29), and all in the hope of at last conceiving a boy. After her seventh girl, she agreed to contraception.

The last census shows that the phenomenon is widespread. There were 117 newborn boys for every 100 girls in the year 2000. A decade earlier, the figures were 112 to 100.

The only hope for girls lies in the cities, there people are better educated and things are slowly evolving in the girls' favour.

Sunday 8 October.
Rain.

Today, I came back to the dormitory with a few other students. I put down what I was carrying. Then I asked my aunt, Ma Shiping, to lend me her exercise book and explain a question to me. She pretended that she didn't understand it either.

I tried to look at her exercise book, but she pulled it away and swore at me.

Once again, I have the feeling that everyone resents me, whereas I don't feel resentful of anybody. Perhaps I'm not seeing things very clearly.

I never lie. I'm not like Ma Shiping, who always tells lies, especially when she's done wrong. I shall have to work even harder so that I never have to ask anyone's help in understanding a question.

Monday 9 October.
A grey day.

This afternoon, we had a Chinese test. The teacher said to us: 'Work quickly and it will soon be over.' My pulse raced. There was a question I didn't know how to answer.

I still haven't solved the problem.

All year long, pupils are subjected to tests which evaluate their progress. Four times a year, in the middle and at the end of each term, they take formal examinations. These stretch over a few days and will determine whether they move into the next grade.

Tension is at its highest at the end of the school year. Very few students are allowed to resit an exam because of a system of catch-up exams. Taking a grade twice over is a terrible loss of face for the student and even more so for the family. Selection becomes even tougher at university entrance time when finals are a real trial for the students.

Music lesson today. But the teacher is away. I fill up my notebook with writing exercises. The class head, Ma Fulu, a very tall boy and one who's nasty to all of us, shouts at me, 'Ma Yan, you ought not to be doing that exercise. This is a music lesson!'

I answer: 'All the others are doing the same thing. Why pick on me?'

He starts to shout. 'I don't give a damn about the others. I'm talking to you!'

I'm furious. When I grow up, I really will go to university and become a policewoman. I vow that I'll fight him then, with no hesitation.

Monday 23 October.
Light rain.

This morning, after classes, I went to the market in Yuwang with two friends. We saw a lot of people there who are very different from us. One doesn't have a leg, another is missing a foot. There's even a blind man.

I used to think I'd never survive in this school. And today, I meet a blind man. A blind man manages to live, so why shouldn't I?

I have to get better and better and get ahead of everyone at school.

Tuesday 24 October.
A fine day.

This afternoon, our music teacher, the one with the long plait, gives us a lesson.

At the end, she asks: 'Who can tell us a story?' Everyone points to Yang Bin, a boy I like a lot. The teacher asks him to come up to the platform, but Yang Bin doesn't manage to get to the end of his story. Hu Zhimin takes over, but he can't finish the story either. The teacher starts where he left off, but even she can't bring it to a conclusion. Finally she tells us another story called 'The Fox Eats the Chicken'. This is a funny story, and I'm drunk with laughter.

Wednesday 25 October.

This afternoon, our Chinese teacher asks us either to sing, to recite a poem or to tell a story.

I particularly liked the song my little brother Ma Yichao sang: 'Wait for the Day when you Say Goodbye'.

We learned this song together when we were in the third year. The words give us courage. 'At the moment when mother and father come to say goodbye, they declare, "Child, I'm sending you on your way. You're no longer to think of your parents or of your beautiful native land."'

I like this song very much because it was Mother herself who taught it to us. When I hear it, I always think of her.

She was the one who made it possible for me go back to school. I need to go to school to get to university and find a good job. Then Mother can have a happy life. She'll be through with this existence where there's never enough to eat. I want my mother to live happily in the second part of her life.

Thursday 26 October.

This afternoon, during break after our first Chinese lesson, we skipped with a rope. Our Chinese teacher, Ma Shixiong, a man of about twenty-seven, who's very nice to us, stood and watched us. His face beamed with happiness, as if he were the same age as us. I haven't seen him this happy since term started.

I think he's reminded of his childhood when he watches us. When he was a child, he probably played the same games, and played them well.

That's why, seeing us skipping, he remembers that happy time and looks so pleased.

Friday 27 October.

We walk home in a light rain which gradually eases.

I have a row with my aunt, Ma Shiping, who is two years older than me and a head taller. She says I'm selfish, that I take other people's things, but when others borrow my school things, I call them copycats.

I reply, 'Didn't you borrow my things? Didn't you take my exercise book? Who did you want to show it to?'

'I didn't take it. It was Xiao Hong,' she answers.

I ask Xiao Hong, but she claims she's got nothing to do with it.

Ma Shiping is upset and says no more.

So I retort, 'You even lie to yourself.'

Saturday 28 October.

This morning the weather was beautiful. But, after a while, the snow started to fall. Blown by the wind, the flakes floated and danced in the sky.

Seeing the snow, I thought of one of my paternal grandmother's sayings: 'If it snows at the beginning of October,[29] the wheat harvest the following year will be good.'

That's why I'm so happy to see snow. Let it snow a lot. The villagers will have water to drink and they won't need to go and fetch it from far away.

---

29 Here the reference is to the lunar calendar which has twelve months of thirty days. The New Year falls in a variable manner between 21 January and 19 February on the Gregorian calendar. Every three years a month is added in order to correct discrepancies between the seasons and holidays. Thus Ma Yan says her birthday is 28 February 1988, which on the Gregorian calendar would be 6 March 1988.

Every family has two cisterns, one for snow, one for rain,
to provide drinkable water.

There is no running water in the village of Zhangjiashu. The villagers have two ways of stocking up. They gather rain and snow water, which they store in cement cisterns dug into the ground and they also have a well of 'bitter water', situated in the valley, an hour's walk from the village. This well is only good for watering the fields or for household tasks. It irritates the skin if you use it for washing, Bai Juhua tells us.

Several times a week, the villagers walk to the well to fetch the bitter water in buckets hanging from a wooden stick balanced on the back of the neck. Children like Ma Yan and her brother can only manage to carry a single bucket home. The buckets are heavy.

According to Ma Yan's mother, it's best to arrive at the well before dawn if you don't want to queue for a long time. This means setting off at about four in the morning. The imam tells us there once used to be a well in the centre of the village but it collapsed and the money isn't available to restore it.

The better-off can buy their water in plastic containers in Yuwang. It costs about fifty yuan, transport included, for two weeks' supply for a family but this is beyond the reach of most of the villagers. In desperate times, the inhabitants go and plead with the commune authorities to send a truck full of drinking water to the village to help them out.

Sunday 29 October.

This morning, it's very cold. I'm off to visit my paternal grand-mother who lives with one of my uncles in the village and I stay for quite a while.

When I get home, Mother starts to reprimand me. 'Why don't you prepare the vegetables you need for school, yourself? You always wait for me to do it. Do you know where those little white rolls you like come from? Have you ever thought about it? I steam them for you and your brother and then the rest of the family is deprived of wheat flour. You know very well we're going through hard times and that I'm ill. And on top of that you want me to wait on you. You're really heartless. I allow you to study but you never think of me once you go to school.'

All of these criticisms come out in any old order and suddenly I'm angry. Other children pay a yuan to get a ride on a tractor to go to school. My brother and I always walk both ways.

But it's also true that we live in want. Without my mother, I would never have been able to go back to school. She doesn't look after her health and she makes it possible for us to study.

I really shall have to make my contribution to the country and have a good career so that my family isn't looked down upon any longer.

Monday 30 October.

This afternoon the last period of the day was a class assembly where all our group's problems were sorted out, either ones to do with study or with health or with communal living.

Ma Ping and Ma Shengliang had had a quarrel. The insults they hurled at each other were painful to listen to. Suddenly the teacher opened the door. A comrade by the name of Hu had told him what was going on. Now the teacher reprimanded both students. They squirmed on their bench, ill at ease, in danger of squashing it under their weight. None of which stopped the teacher from continuing his severe criticism.

I think he's right. In order for there not to be any more quarrels or out-and-out fights, this is the best thing he can do to ensure the good behaviour of the entire class.

Tuesday 31 October.

This afternoon our music teacher taught us a new song, 'The Sun'. Then she asked us to sing everything we'd learned since our first lesson. When we had finished, she asked if anyone would like to sing alone. Everyone said that my little brother, Ma Yichao, sang very well.

I'm so pleased for him. I'm proud of having a talented brother, especially since I can't sing. Ma Yichao, who has a roguish manner, with his short hair and laughing eyes, is known throughout the school for his songs. Whenever anyone asks for a singer, the answer is invariably: 'Ma Yan's brother'.

My heart is full of joy, like a flower whose petals are opening.

Monday 1 November.

It's a beautiful day. We're having a nature class. The natural sciences teacher reminds me of a teacher I had in my second year of primary school. Their attitudes and gestures are very similar. When I see my current teacher, it makes me think of all the little attentions my old teacher paid me. So that I would have a good voice, he taught me to sing. So that I would be in good health, he had me do sport.

Thursday 2 November.

Chinese lesson this morning. The teacher hasn't prepared anything and he asks us to read the text ourselves. He picks Ma Chengmin, Ma Shilong and Ma Shengliang. But these comrades don't quite manage to read the whole text. The teacher then chooses Li Xiaoyan. She reads beautifully. Mandarin[30] on her lips is lovely to listen to.

The teacher calls on my brother twice, each time to answer a single question. He performs well and manages to answer both. My anxiety is stilled. I was afraid my brother might make mistakes.

The teacher asks Bai Xue what 'pretend' and 'never to know' mean. Bai Xue answers. My pulse is racing. I'm worrying that I'll be next. I haven't even managed to finish my thought when the teacher asks me to stand up. He asks: 'Into how many parts can

---

30 Mandarin is the Chinese national language but each region, indeed each town, has its own language or dialect – Cantonese, Shanghaian, Hakka, etc. These can be very different from the national language, to the point where it's incomprehensible to other Chinese. Thus, for instance, the people of Hong Kong, who were long cut off from mainland China during the colonial period, speak Cantonese and do not understand a word of Mandarin. Ningxia has its own regional language and certain teachers use it in their classes at Ma Yan's school.

lesson twelve be divided?' I answer, 'Into three parts: first, the preparation for writing the letter; second, writing the letter; third, the sending of the letter.'

I fear that my answer may be wrong, but the teacher says, 'Correct,' and I unwind a little. But the teacher continues to question me. 'Is there anything else?' I give the right answer, and he says, 'Correct, but you need to read the text some more.'

Friday 3 November.

This afternoon, my brother and I went home.

It's very cold and when we get there, no one's in. A neighbour tells us my mother went to see our paternal grandfather. My fifth uncle,[31] a man who's as tall as my father and who has had seven daughters, is building a house. My brother and I put on the padded jackets which keep us very warm and go off to our grandfather's.

A lot of people are gathered to help build the house.[32] The wind is so strong, it's hard to keep our eyes open. We go into the house. Mother is busy cooking. She gives us two bowls of vegetables and tells us to eat up.

A little later, my grandfather comes in too. Mother gives him a bowl as well. Grandpa sits down on a stool and starts to eat. His eyes are full of tears from the wind. His cotton jacket and his shirt are so dirty, it's best not to look at them. When I look at my grandmother, I think that she's even more pitiful than he is. Her hair is all white, a towel full of holes covers her head. As well as this, she's carrying two of the daughters of my fifth uncle in her arms. The children kick against her hard.

---

31 The fifth uncle refers to her father's youngest brother.
32 Houses are built through a system of mutual aid. Every villager helps everyone else in the work of construction.

How can Grandmother bear it? How her arms must ache . . . In her place, I'd be in agony.

If I manage to get through my studies and find work, I'll certainly take my grandparents into my house, so that they can lead a happier life. Then they won't have to put up with fifth uncle's constant bad temper. I just fear they won't be able to hold on that long. But that would mean that they're condemned to a miserable old age, without ever having had the chance to lead a good life.

'My life is very hard,' Ma Shunji, Ma Yan's grandfather, says. His opening words do little to prepare us for what follows.

Despite the fact that he's eighty, and is wearing an outmoded, thickly padded jacket, Ma Shunji holds himself very straight. A sparse beard protrudes from his chin. His face is lined. On his head is the white cotton hat that Chinese Muslims wear.

A native of the district of Xiji, further south, Ma Shunji's father was a beggar who went from village to village begging alms. When he was a child, Ma Shunji accompanied him. But when he turned four, his father sold him for two kilos of rice and a handful of seeds to a rich landowner from Zhangjiashu who had no children of his own.

Ma Yan's grandfather worked on the farm from the age of seven on, which wasn't exceptional at that time in the countryside. At the age of twenty, in the midst of the civil war in China, he was given up by his adoptive parents, who in the meantime had had three children of their own, to the Kuomintang army of Chang Kai-Shek. The nationalist party demanded of each large family a man fit to fight the Communists. According to family legend, Ma Shunji's adoptive father offered the Kuomintang officer, who had tied Ma Shunji behind his horse, a bribe of a bottle of wine to kill the youth on the way to war. That way he wouldn't be forced to give up another son to the Kuomintang army. Any family who lost a man during active service was exempt from further conscription.

Apparently the officer took pity on Ma Shunji and he fought alongside him for six years. Then, after quarrelling with his fellow officers, he deserted. He crossed the Yellow River and joined Mao's Communist insurgents on the other side.

By 1949, Mao's army had sent the Kuomintang into retreat on the island of Taiwan and had established itself as the government on the Chinese mainland. It is understandable that Ma Yan's family would want to insist that Grandfather fought with the Red Army rather than on his participation, however modest, in the nationalist cause. There was a time in China's history when even this minor blot on a person's past could have tragic consequences.

The years of active duty weren't over for Ma Shunji. In 1950, he was posted as a 'volunteer' to the neighbouring Korean peninsula to fight the Americans. During his twelve years of service, he never had a single leave that permitted him to return to his village. Only with the end of the Korean War, in 1953, did he return. He came on the back of a donkey, his only recompense being a hero's medal on his chest and a red paper flower in his buttonhole.

On the eve of his departure from his village, he had been married off to a thirteen-year-old girl who, like him, was an orphan sold off to a large family that mistreated her. She was still waiting for him, even though she could barely remember the face of the man she had spent a single night with twelve years earlier. In all that time she had not received a word of news of him.

She had remained faithful to him, even though the officials had told her that her husband was probably dead, like all the others who hadn't reappeared after the Communist victory of 1949. She had resisted later offers of marriage. She was still hoping for the miracle that ultimately came about. When she asked Ma Shunji why he hadn't written in all those years, he replied simply: 'I can't write.'

She asked him, then, if he still wanted her as his wife. He said he'd had some 'sentimental attachments' in Korea, that he could easily have remarried there, but that he had come back for her.

Almost fifty years later, they are still living together in Zhangjiashu, after having had five boys, one of which is Ma Yan's father.

This morning Father came back from far away.[33] I suggested that I make a meal for him, but he said no. He had to go and help the fifth uncle build his house. He went out straight away. There's only my brother and me in the house. I put a low table on the *kang* and do my homework there.

My little brother is playing outside. A little while later, other children come and play with him and then go away. When I've finished my work, I go and look for my brother. Hu Xiaoping, the son of a neighbour, tells me that he went off to the fifth uncle's house. I sit around for a bit, but then I get so bored that I go off there too. Father and a lot of the other villagers work until nightfall. Then the others clamber down the house frame, eat and go back home.

Only my father and my little brother are still at work. They carry on until nine o'clock. Why don't they stop? I ask.

The fifth aunt, Uncle's wife, answers me: 'Your father only arrived at noon so he hasn't done much work. And here you are telling him to stop already.'

I should have replied, 'Last year when we built our house, you only came to help in the afternoons. Did we say anything? You don't even know how to tell good from bad. You and us, we're not the same. We're not the same at all.'

But I didn't say a word.

33 Ma Yan's father had been away for three months working on a construction site in Hohhot, capital of Inner Mongolia, several hundred kilometres away. But at the end of his stint, he was cheated out of his money and never paid. Since they have no legal status, migrant workers have no recourse to justice when something like this happens. 'He didn't even have the money for his train fare home,' his wife told us.

Sunday 5 November.

This afternoon, we were still at home, even though we should have been on our way to school. But our little bread rolls weren't ready. My brother and I decided to leave in any case and locked the door. We went to find Father in the village, to give him the key, and he advised us to wait until we'd eaten before leaving. I told him Ma Shiping said we had to leave early today because we might be able to hitch a ride on a tractor.

My brother says he's hungry and thirsty. He sits down and waits for something to eat. My father gives me ten yuan to buy some bread with. I run into a shop to get change for the money and give five yuan back to my father. The rest will be enough for bread.

I suddenly think that it has taken my father such hard work to earn these yuan. He's given his sweat and blood for them, working in Inner Mongolia. How can I take them just on a whim? I must work harder and make it to university, so as to get proper work. Then I'll never again be weighed down and saddened by these questions of money.

Monday 6 November.

This afternoon, I'm busy reading my Chinese manual when the bell rings to announce the end of the period. All my friends go out to play. A little while later, several of them come back to say that there's going to be a Chinese test. My heart starts racing. People are getting their books out to look through them because the questions in the test will certainly be there somewhere. And then someone claims otherwise. The test will be on a wholly different subject and on a separate sheet of paper.

I don't trust myself, so I carry on studying the book.

The lesson starts. The teacher comes in, empty-handed. He says we're going to have a class reunion instead of a test. I'm so happy. Full of joy like a bud blossoming into flower. I'm no longer afraid.

Tuesday 7 November.

Music lesson this afternoon. The teacher gives us a new song to learn, 'Little Tadpole'. It's a lovely song. 'Little tadpole, big head, tiny body, small tail, lives in the water and grows until he's utterly transformed.'

The teacher sings it a few times with us, then asks us to sing it without her. We sing in chorus for a few minutes, then the teacher asks us to sing one by one. 'Who's a good singer?' she asks, and the pupils all shout out in unison, 'Li Xiaoyan, Bai Xue, Ma Zhonghong, and Ma Xiaojun.'

The teacher with the long plait asks my brother, Ma Yichao: 'Why don't you sing for your comrades? What do you all think?' Everyone approves.

My brother gets up and sings. He's very funny and everyone bursts into laughter. He isn't the person he used to be. He's become a comedian. He tells funny stories. He likes playing the clown.

In this school we only learn one song a week. 'Little Tadpole' is the one I like singing most of all.

Wednesday 8 November.

It's beautiful this morning. My father came from the village and brought bread for my brother and for me. After class, I went to the market with my brother. My father's already there waiting for us. I ask him why he asked us to meet him here. He says he wants us to have one very good meal.

He takes us to one of the little restaurants on Yuwang's main street, orders two bowls of rice cooked in a meat soup, and tells us to eat. Afterwards, he also buys us some apples, stipulating that we're to eat them with our evening bread.

On the road back to school, I meet my great-uncle and his wife, my second uncle and his wife, my third uncle and my maternal grandfather. They say to me: 'So you went to market too.' I say yes.

They don't invite my brother and me to eat with them. I think about this. How good it is to have parents! Without parents, you're an orphan and there's no one to take care of you and love you.

How wonderful it is to have parents and their love!

Thursday 9 November.

This afternoon, it's beautiful out. Our last class is the natural sciences one. Everyone rushes in when it begins. But my aunt, Ma Shiping, and I drag our feet for a bit in the courtyard. I see the teacher arriving and I rush like a mad thing and get into the classroom just behind him.

The moment I come in, the other children get up to greet the teacher. I rush to my place so as not to miss anything. After the class, the teacher distributes our notebooks and assigns the homework for the next lesson. He adds, 'When you've finished, don't leave the room. Your Chinese teacher still has a few things to say to you.'

I fear that we may be having a surprise test. But, in fact, it's only so that we can do an exercise in our workbooks. He warns us that tomorrow morning the inspectors will be coming round to examine our work.

Friday 10 November.

This afternoon we made the trek home after school. My mother was preparing noodles for my brother and me. My father was outside, busy mixing water with coal dust. With the mud it makes, we create coal cakes to burn.

My brother and I went off to visit our paternal grandmother, who lives at the fifth uncle's. My grandparents live in the big room. My uncle has dug a sort of cave next to the house for his seven children.

When we arrive, our grandmother is out. Our cousin tells us that our grandparents are busy cutting fodder for the ox. We go off to help them. When he's finished cutting the grass, Grandfather feeds it to the ox. Grandmother invites us into the kitchen and offers us bread and steamed potatoes. I accept half a roll and my brother has a potato.

My grandmother's hair is all white. She's almost eighty but she still works for fifth uncle's family. So does my grandfather who's the same age. Old people who have an education certainly don't have to do this kind of work. Surely when one reaches old age, it's time to benefit from life. Nowhere but here do you see old people serving the young like this.

It's obvious that one has to study these days in order to avoid the fate of my grandparents, who have to slave away into their old age. They'll never taste happiness.

Ma Yan with her paternal grandparents.

Saturday 11 November.

It's very cold this afternoon. My father comes back from the market. He puts his bags on the ground and climbs up on the *kang*. Sitting on the bed, he grumbles, 'It really is very cold today! So cold you can't take your hands out of your pockets.'

I ask him what's in the bags. My little brother, Ma Yiting, jumps off the bed to go and look. He sees a padded jacket, a pullover and some coloured tiles for the house. He asks who the jacket and the pullover belong to and my father says, 'They're for your sister and your big brother.'

My youngest brother then starts to cry. My father promises him that on the next market day, he'll buy one for him. Reassured, the little one stops crying. Then my mother reproaches him severely for asking for things from his father, and Ma Yiting starts crying again.

My mother must be suffering from her stomach pains today. Otherwise, why chide the little one like that?

Sunday 12 November.

This afternoon, my aunt, Ma Shiping, my brother Ma Yichao and I were all on our way to school together when we were stopped at the intersection of Hujiashu village by five or six big boys who asked us where we were going.

My brother answered that we were going to school in Yuwang.

'What year are you in?' they asked.

'Why do you want to know?' my brother retorted.

These boys were not from our village and suddenly they grew aggressive. The youngest of them threw stones at us. The biggest hurled insults. We started to run as fast as we could until we got to the ravine. There we saw some shepherds tending their flocks. Once again, I grew very frightened. But when I looked at the shepherds more closely, I could see they were adults. I calmed down.

My palms were damp, as if I'd just come out of the water.

Monday 13 November.

It's a beautiful afternoon and our final period is devoted to a class assembly. The teacher asks the student responsible for our communal life to organise us in such a way that the school is kept thoroughly clean. The head boy tells the boys to sweep the yard, and the girls to clean the windows. Ma Jing, Ma Donghong and Li Qing sweep the yard. I let them do it and then clean up the dust.

Every time I pick up a broom and a dustpan, I think of my family. We clean the floor in the same way. I remember the first time my mother taught me to sweep. She explained: 'When you sweep the ground, it's best to sprinkle it with a bit of water first, then you wait a moment before beginning.' Mother held my two hands. She advised me to bend a little at the waist. That way I wouldn't make the dust fly.

I remember each of her words as if they were spoken yesterday.

Tuesday 14 November.

Another beautiful afternoon. Our last lesson is music. The teacher comes in and the head boy barks: 'Get up. Good afternoon, teacher.'

The teacher replies, 'Good afternoon, comrades.'[34] Sit down. Today, we're going to learn 'At the Sound of the Little Drum'.

---

34 This expression, which has Communist resonances, is also used by the students to and about each other.

The teacher repeats the song several times, then asks us to sing. We sing badly, so she repeats it again. Then she says, 'You'll sing it again after class. That way you'll know it well.'

She also says, 'I heard that you would soon have your mid-term exam. Is that right?'

All the comrades answer, 'Yes.'

The music teacher allows us to revise our work so that we get good results the next day. When I hear her give us permission to do this, it's as if I'd received a dose of mother-love.

Wednesday 15 November.

It's snowing hard this afternoon. In our first period, the maths teacher comes in and announces, 'Today, we'll be taking the mid-term exam.' My heart sets up a hammering.

We have to solve problems and fill in the blanks. For the most part, it seems quite easy to me.

The teacher announces: 'I read, you write.' As we go on, the problems get harder and harder. I'm no longer able to fill in some of the blanks. Nor can I even do a simple calculation. I do the best I can.

After class, I compare my answers to those of others. But none of my answers correspond.

Mother, all the hope you've put in me has been in vain. I'll try and give you more satisfaction later on, okay, Mother? I promise. I'll try and get better results in future.

Thursday 16 November.

Our first two classes are in Chinese grammar and spelling. The teacher explains: 'You'll revise during the next two lessons and then next week, you'll sit your Chinese exam.'

This makes me think of yesterday's exam. When the teacher

distributed the papers, at first glance everything looked simple. So I started to answer the questions. But towards the end I ran into more and more problems.

No sooner had the Chinese teacher uttered the word 'exam' than I no longer had the heart to carry on reading my book. Do you want to know why? Yesterday I went to the office of the maths teacher. His niece and his two twin daughters were just looking over my paper, corrected by the teacher. I had got eight answers wrong. There were not that many questions altogether, and I got eight of them wrong! I can hardly be light-hearted after that.

I also saw Bai Xue's paper. I had the feeling that I was the lowest of the low and she had walked the heavens. What distance there was between us. It was as if I had never existed.

Friday 17 November.

When night falls, Mother heats up some water and tells me to wash my hair. My paternal grandmother, she explains, is ill. She's got pains in her kidneys and her legs. My two brothers have gone off to see her.

When the water is finally hot, I wash my hair. My brother, Ma Yichao, comes home alone, his hands covering his face.

Mother asks him, 'Did you really go to Grandmother's? You saw her?'

'No,' he replies.

'Why ever not?'

He explains. 'Grandfather had been to the mosque at Liwazi, two kilometres from the village. They'd given him a present of meat pancakes. When Ma Yiting and I reached his door, he shouted at us. "It's so cold outside. Why on earth have you come?"'

There was little point in repeating that they'd come to see their grandmother. He sent them away because, he said, it was so cold. So my brothers came home.

Mother starts to criticise Grandfather. 'How can we look after him if he behaves like that?'

But I think she's wrong. Grandfather will never change. He doesn't understand that we want the best for him. When my mother criticises him, I feel terrible. Why do none of his daughters-in-law understand what's going on inside him? He's always been like this. I hope I'll never hear another disagreeable comment about my grandfather.

Saturday 18 November.

It's very cold this afternoon. The snow is falling thickly and there's a gusting wind. Father came back from market where he bought two bags of wheat. He's also got other things which he's carried in a big sack. He comes into the room and puts down his bundle. Mother takes out the vegetables, garlic, noodles. She looks right down into the bottom of the bag, where she finds one or two kilos of meat. She asks Father why he thought it was a good idea to buy meat. He explains: 'Today the children are all home together. Let's have a feast. They don't eat well at school. That's why I bought a little meat for them.'

So Mother makes a soup with rice and meat for us. While we're eating, she comes out with one of her sayings. 'Liver isn't meat. A nephew isn't a descendant. The son must give birth to himself. The tree must have deep roots.'

No matter how much I think about the meaning of these phrases, I understand nothing at all.[35]

---

35 What Bai Juhua's saying means is that one's own children are the most important thing for a man or a woman.

Sunday 19 November.

This afternoon, just before we have to leave for school, my brother Ma Yichao recounts what happened to us last Friday on our way home; how we were attacked by five youths from another village. After she's listened to us, Mother asks Father, who hasn't gone off to his work outside the village yet, to accompany us. Father hoists our provisions on his shoulder. We each take our schoolbag, but I'm also carrying my brother's clothes and shoes.

We set off on our long trudge of several hours through the snow. When we get to the top of the plateau, Father's ears are already very red. We're walking in silence. I hear his tread and I see the snow on his leather shoes.

I think of my exam results. How can I possibly merit the long walk Father is making for our sakes? He's afraid we'll be beaten up on the way. I'm going to study harder now, be successful, then go off to university and find work. I must pay Father back for this walk and give him and Mother the gift of a better life.

Monday 20 November.

This morning our first lesson is a study period where we can do our homework and read over our texts. The Chinese teacher warns us: 'Revise your lessons well. Our next period will be the Chinese exam.'

All the comrades launch themselves into revision. When the time for the next period arrives, the teacher comes into the classroom and distributes the exam papers. I can see that it's easy and I settle right in. While I'm writing, I tell myself that I absolutely must do well for Mother and Father's sake and get a top grade.

The time comes to hand in our exam papers. I ask the others how many ticks they had – that is affirmative answers – and how many crosses – the negative answers. They say three crosses and one tick. Does that mean I've once again made mistakes? Mother and Father's hope vanishes into the distance once more.

I shall have to study more in order to do justice to my parents.

Tuesday 21 November.

The last lesson this afternoon is music. The teacher writes out the lyrics to songs on the blackboard. The first is called, 'I Have a Sheep'. While the teacher writes, she leans her head against the blackboard, as if she's ill. It's clear that she has a headache. Writing is a strain and she barely gets through all the stanzas.

The second song is 'Wooden Rattles'. The teacher gives the songsheet to Hu Zhimin and asks him to write it out for her. She sits down. I don't know what's wrong with her, but she seems very unwell. She looks as if she could pass out at any moment.

Hu Zhimin has copied out the words on the board and the teacher gives us the tune. Then she asks us to sing on our own. We don't quite get to the end. She makes us repeat it all several times, then confides, 'Ma Huiping, in class three of the fifth year, sings really well.'

The true meaning of this, from what I can gather, is that we should try and follow her example.

The teacher has worn herself out on the platform and we still can't sing the whole song. It's not fair on her. Despite her illness, she's come to teach us so that we can take our turn in the revolutionary celebrations later on.

On the afternoon of 21 November all the Pioneers at the school celebrated the anniversary of President Mao Zedong's saying[37] invoking us to follow the example of Grandfather Jin Zhanlin.[38] In order to celebrate the spirit of Jin Zhanlin who helped others, in order to learn what his good works meant and so that we contribute our own heart of love, we must

1 Give books to other young comrades, so that they too learn from the example of grandfather Jin Zhanlin and do good;
2 Learn to do housework and help our parents;
3 Conscientiously protect public property.

All the Young Pioneers in the school need to follow the example of Jin Zhanlin and offer up their love. If we live, it's in order to improve the lives of others.

All the Young Pioneers of the school
21 November

36 This letter of Ma Yan's is part of her activity as a Young Pioneer. Children are often seen sporting the red neckties of the Pioneers.
37 All the speeches and proclamations of the 'Great Helmsman', as Mao was known, were the object of 'sayings' gathered together in the Little Red Book, which not so very long ago all Chinese people had to learn by heart.
38 A local hero who died several years ago, Jin Zhanlin was a model electrician who, according to Maoist myth, gave free and willing service to the residents of Yuwang. In the tradition of Lei Feng, this soldier in the popular struggle served as an example to the Chinese people. The propaganda of the 1960s had him sewing holes in his comrades' socks, a veritable saint of self-abnegation.

Wednesday 22 November.

The last class of the day is given up to the activities of the Young Pioneers. Hu Zhimin is the organiser. He picks out names at random. He asks my aunt, Ma Shiping, to get up and sing. At first she refuses. I'm pleased, because she made fun of me and said I sing like a little pig. Today, when the teacher asks her, she sings, but she's worse than I am.

When my turn comes, the teacher asks me to sing, 'The Dream Butterfly':

> *Beautiful butterfly of my dream*
> *fly amongst others*
> *fly through the pretty flowers . . .*

All the comrades say I've sung well, and that I could become a star . . .

Secretly, I'm very pleased. As of today, I've got more confidence in my ability to sing. I shall have to carry on and do even better. I don't want to hear others insinuate that I sing like a pig.

Thursday 23 November.

I'm busy correcting a text this afternoon when the school day comes to an end. My young brother, Ma Yichao, brings food and calls me to come and eat.

A lot of comrades confide their admiration to me: 'How kind your brother is! He brings you food and lets you eat first. He eats your leftovers. After your meal, he goes to get water so that you can wash your bowl . . .'

I'm so pleased by their words.

But today my brother has only brought rice without any vegetables. Halfway through the meal, my aunt, Ma Shiping, gives me a spoonful of her vegetables. I take a mouthful and give the rest to my brother.

At that moment, I suddenly understand the true meaning of a sense of family. What the love of a mother is.

Friday 24 November.

Before lunch, my father and mother came to school to see my brother and me. They brought us a little rice and asked us to give it to our main teacher, that is, our Chinese teacher.

The bell announcing class rings. When lessons are over, my brother and I race down the road, but my parents are already leaving to see our maternal grandmother. They've heard she's still ill, which is why they want to go and see her. They give me a yuan to buy some apples to have with our evening bread.

Today, I'm very sad. Do you want to know why? Because this morning my parents told me that when I got home, I had to feed the ox. I refused. But when I got home, I did feed the ox. The work has left my hands all rough and swollen.[39] They're horrible to look at. And so I'm led to reflect: I've fed the ox once and my hands are already rough. Mother feeds him every day – which explains why her hands are so swollen. Everything she does is for my brothers' and my future.

I want to cry and can't say a word. Please come back, Mother and Father. I need your love! I was wrong, okay? Come back quick. I'm thinking of you. Please come back.

39 Ma Yan's hands are swollen because the ox's food takes a long time to mix up and knead.

Saturday 25 November.

My parents said they would be back from my maternal grandparents' today. My brothers and I got up very early. We prepared the food for the ox. Then I cooked for all of us. After we'd eaten, we stayed on the *kang* to watch a television series. After that, we went out to play.

Soon after that, the sun set behind the mountain. But Father and Mother still didn't appear. We made some supper for ourselves and ate. After that, my brothers stayed at home to watch a cartoon, but I was worried so I went out, without quite knowing where I was going.

Seeing me in this state, my brother went to find the second uncle's daughter, so that she could keep us company. We chatted for a bit, then my brothers and I went to bed without saying another word.

A house without grown-ups doesn't feel normal. Children are always children. My father and mother have gone to see the maternal grandparents and I feel desperate. I hope they come back soon.

Sunday 26 November.

This afternoon when we got to school, the dormitory was still locked. Only Ma Juan is there, a friend from our class. We sit down in front of the dormitory. After a while, another comrade arrives, Ma Yuehua. She asks us why we don't go in. We tell her the door is still locked. She has the key, she tells us. We go in and put down our bags. We open our books and start to read.

A little while later a motorbike,[40] driven by a man, pulls up outside.

---

40 A motorbike is a coveted possession in this region, since it is particularly well adapted for the distances between villages and the narrow roads so often worn away by rain which makes travel by car or tractor difficult. Because only a few civil servants and business people can afford them, a great deal of value and status resides in a motorbike.

Yang Xiaohua has been given a lift all the way to school. Both of them come to the dormitory.

The man asks, 'Is your stove working?'

'No,' we answer.

He asks us why we don't light the coal stove.

'The hearth is too full,' we explain.

He takes off his jacket and starts to clean out all of last week's ashes. I ask myself who this man could be and why he's busying himself with getting our stove going. It turns out he's Yang Xiaohua's father. He's a nice man. When he dies, he'll certainly go to heaven.

Of course, this is only in my imagination . . .

Monday 27 November.

This afternoon, the last session is given up to a class meeting. The teacher asks us to clean the school. Some comrades concentrate on the yard, others simply play. I do some revision in the classroom. The student responsible for communal life comes in to tell me to go out. I go. During my absence, the floor is swept. I return to the classroom and carry on with my homework. He calls me again, this time to tell me to clean the windows. I go out and start wiping them. After that, I return to the classroom once more.

He calls me yet again to tell me to go and do some dusting elsewhere. When I don't answer, he comes up close and smacks me. I still don't say anything. He hits me harder and harder. I pick up my little ruler and hit him across the face. Then I go off to do the dusting. I'm furious. If I become a good policewoman tomorrow and this boy commits a crime, I'll arrest him and shoot him. I'll cut him up with a knife!

Tuesday 28 November.

Mother and Father, forgive me. Why do I ask for your forgiveness straight away? Because this afternoon, the Chinese teacher, the most important one, lectured us: 'Last week, you sat your mid-term exams. Several comrades performed very well, but the vast majority of you had very poor results. You, the boarders, every week you bring a bag of rolls with you and once a term, a sack of rice: do you think you deserve as much? Not even bread and rice. As for the rest of you . . .'

When the teacher gives out the exam results, I can't lift my head. I haven't even come second. Will I ever be able to hold my head high again?

But I have to be confident. In the finals, I'll certainly have better results to show my parents.

Wednesday 29 November.

This morning the maths teacher came in with thirty-seven workbooks in his hand. The atmosphere is bizarre. It really is. The teacher takes a handful of these exercise books and starts in: 'I've already told you that you haven't done the necessary work, there's no point handing it in!'

The top notebook belongs to Li Qing. The teacher asks her to get up and leave the class. She refuses. The teacher slaps her with the back of his hand across the neck. Then he slaps each of us one after another.[41] He has a last exercise book in his hand. It belongs to Ma Fulu. The teacher orders him forward and, without saying a word, hits him.

I'm secretly very happy about this, because Ma Fulu has hit other comrades. And today, it's the teacher's turn to slap him. He knows

41 Ma Yan wasn't punished that day.

now what it feels like, knows just how pleasant it is! Might he now give up his habit of roughing up others? I so hope he'll never hit us again.[42]

Thursday 30 November.

Chinese class this morning. As soon as the teacher comes in, he asks if anyone present has any glass marbles. These are not allowed in school. The class head indicates one comrade, then another and another. The teacher confiscates a whole handful of marbles before at last beginning the lesson.

Lesson 22: The Golden Bait: a war narrative. The teacher announces that he's going to read the text and that we'll then analyse its meaning. While the teacher reads, I can't hold back my tears. Because my grandfather is just like one of these Red Army veterans who's come back from the anti-American war in Korea. He, too, crossed the steppes, climbed mountains of snow.[43] In fact, he resembles the old squadron chief quoted by our teacher – a man who persevered until the ultimate victory.

I'm proud of him and my tears flow in homage to his bravery.

42 Once, Ma Yan tells us, a child had a bit of ear ripped off. There is no recourse to a higher authority, either for pupils or for their parents.
    Part of the problem lies with the teachers' own lack of training. The majority in the rural areas have no teaching qualification. The state is slowly trying to improve the quality of teaching, but it's a slow process, and lacks the necessary investment.
43 Originally an expression used to describe the hardships of the Long March undertaken by Mao and his partisans during the 1930s.

Ma Yan's paternal grandfather Ma Shunji served in the long and difficult Korean War (1950–53). He was a Chinese 'volunteer' sent by Mao to fight at the side of Korean Communist comrades against the Americans and their allies. The old man remembers being encircled by enemy troops and, when food and water ran out, drinking his horse's urine, before killing and eating the animal. He speaks of that time with great emotion, even though his family must have heard his stories thousands of times. A half-century later, he also still remembers some Korean words: 'cook', 'eat' . . .

Several hundreds of thousands of Chinese 'volunteers', up to a million according to some estimates, were killed during the Korean War, which can be seen as the first battle of the long Cold War.

Family photos framed on the wall of the single room in the house.

Friday 1 December.

This afternoon after school, it was very cold. My brother and I got our bags and went to the market. When we arrived, there were no tractors going to our village. We looked around a little longer, and I finally spied a tractor that came from our village. We got up into the trailer at the back. I thought to myself that it was easy enough getting in, but it would be harder getting out, because we would have to pay.

My parents didn't come to town today. Neither my brother nor I have any money. That's why it'll be difficult.

I've barely finished thinking this, when Mother approaches without our knowing. She murmurs, 'You're dying of cold, aren't you?'

I turn round and see her. I'm thrilled. As soon as Mother gets on, the tractor takes off.

On the road, the wind is very strong. My cheeks are bright red. Mother puts her hands on them. Right away, I feel heat coming through.

Mother is being so attentive. When I think of my exam results, I don't know how I'm going to tell her.

At dusk, when the fast is over,[44] we're all watching a cartoon on the television: 'Sun Child'. I go out to see what Mother is up to. I pull back the curtain on the door and see that she's making little potato dumplings for our dinner. I return to watch more of the cartoon with my brothers.

A little while later, I want to go and help Mother. But she's already finished preparing the vegetables and rolls. There's only the rice left to cook.

'Can I help, Mother?' I ask.

'It's not worth it. Better go and do your homework.'

I go back to do some writing.

While I write, I think: what a lot of trouble our parents go to for us. And couldn't we go to just a little trouble for them? So that they can have happy times in which they'll be the ones to be looked after by others.

---

44 As part of her Muslim beliefs, Ma Yan honours the fast of Ramadan.

Although many of Ma Yan's schoolmates are also Hui Muslims, she is one of the few who observes the fast of Ramadan. Before going to her town school, she took instruction from the local imam in a kind of Koranic infants' school, where, she remembers, 'we spent our time singing.' Ma Yan's family, while not particularly religious, respects tradition. Her mother wears the white headscarf of the Huis, as do almost all the women of the village. She also forbids her daughter to wear skirts or to show her bare arms.

At their house, there are no religious symbols – no pictures of Mecca, no Koranic verses on the walls – which is the practice in more pious households. Respecting Ramadan and other holidays associated with it are the only suggestions of religious observance in Ma Yan's journal.

The imam, Hu Dengshuang, one of the important men in the village.

Sunday 3 December.

This afternoon I washed my hair and got ready to go. Mother asked us to stay till the end of the afternoon. At the big mosque in Liwazi, two kilometres away, and in the little one, just behind us, prayers are going on to mark the end of the fast. If we wait, we can get something to eat before heading off.

We stay and sit on the bed. Suddenly I hear someone calling me. It's my aunt, Ma Shiping, who's asking whether we're ready to go. I suggest she comes in and waits with us, so that we can eat.

Mother has our cases ready, and after having served out the food orders us straight off. It's already dark.

The moment we leave, I feel very sad. Tears stream down my face. I'm desolate about leaving home.

On the black, night-time track, I fall behind. A little further on, the other two decide on an alternative route, saying that on the first we might get stopped. I follow them. After we've walked a little more, my brother, Ma Yichao, suggests that next time we should get a tractor for one yuan. I agree. Ma Shiping doesn't. She wants to carry on walking to school.

We trail behind her. It's so dark that after a little while we lose sight of her. We run to catch up with her, but we still can't see her. I start to cry loudly. When we finally find her, I'm so happy, I burst into laughter.

Ma Shiping refuses to be intimidated by potential danger. She won't give in to it. Even if her life is at stake, she carries on. I admire her with all my heart.

Monday 4 December.

Today, after school, the others went home. Ma Jing and I did our homework quickly, then went to the market. In a little shop, I bought a notebook for my Chinese class and a smaller one for my diary. Ma Jing bought a few hairpins and a towel.

By chance I meet a relative, holding a big bag in her hand. She tells me my mother asked her to bring us some padded clothes which would keep us really warm. I open the bag and see that Mother has also sent along some doughnuts cooked in the fat from yesterday's feast.

I'm thrilled. Tonight I'll be able to eat lots. But I ask myself whether we'll be able to return my mother's kindness when she gets old.

Let's hope so . . .

Tuesday 5 December.

Music lesson this afternoon. The teacher warns us: 'Revise well, because next week we're having a test.' Everyone starts to revise. My heart sinks. As soon as the word 'exam' is mentioned, I feel like crying.

Why cry? Because I didn't come top of the class in maths or Chinese in the mid-term exams. When I told my parents about this, Father didn't say anything. He simply walked out of the house. But Mother exploded. 'If you carry on doing badly like this, you won't even deserve the rolls you take along each week.'

Even though Father didn't say anything, I think he's angrier than Mother. That's why I have to do well in the music test next week. I have to bring at least one good grade home to my parents.

Wednesday 6 December.

This morning, it's beautiful out. Beginning the day's fast for Ramadan, the girls in the dorm tell each other funny stories. We've lit the incense we all bought together and we watch it burning. We tell each other we can soon go home and ask our mothers to make us noodles and rolls, so that we don't go around starving all the time.

When I hear a comrade say this, I feel really bad. It reminds me that I didn't come top of the class. How will I be able to face going home and eating the meals Mother prepares?

But I have confidence in myself. At the end-of-term exams, if I don't come first, I must at least come second.

Thursday 7 December.

The last class of the day is natural sciences. Then the comrades go out to play. I stay back to do my homework. Suddenly Ma Xiaohong and my aunt, Ma Shiping, who are in my class, come in and ask, 'What are you up to?'

Ma Xiaohong doesn't move, but Ma Shiping tears the notebook out from under me while I'm still writing. The word scrawls off, the notebook is torn, the pencil broken.

I'm so angry I can't keep it back. I swear at her, insult her. She pays me back in kind. I get so furious I can't even speak any longer. She goes away.

Ma Jing says: 'Your aunt is in a rage.'

I answer, 'Too bad. It's her fault in any case!'

But in my heart, it's as if I'm the guilty one, because she's older than me and I owe her some respect. My explosion was over the top. That's probably why I feel I'm in the wrong.

Friday 8 December.

This afternoon after school, Ma Shiping, my brother and I get ready to put our things away and go off to the market. We see several tractors from our village. We decide to have a look round first, but when we come back, there isn't a single tractor left. We run through all the streets. My brother is in a rage. He starts swearing. We carry on looking for a vehicle, but then my brother disappears, so we have to look for him. We finally find him and also a tractor which comes from not too far away from our village. All three of us get up on the little trailer behind.

The driver's father asks us to divide ourselves up into three tractors. 'You can't all stay here with us. Where will the petrol come from? We're the ones who pay.'

These words make me see red. I'd like to jump off and look for another ride, but there is no other tractor around. I have to stay put and listen to the man.

The tractor heads off and the noise of the engine drowns his voice. I can't hear him any more. I lower my head and end up falling asleep. When I wake up, we're almost home.

When we get off, I take a yuan out of my bag and give it to the driver's father. He looks at us with contempt.

I think to myself, 'Don't take all of us for poor penniless people. Some pupils are rich, some poor. And don't take me for a nobody. If I have to answer back and stand up for myself, I will. Don't mistake all students for people who don't know how to respond to insults, or how to fight. I'm not like the others. If someone offends me, I'll remember his name for ever. I'll never forget.'

Saturday 9 December.

Tonight we got up before daybreak to eat and start our fast for the day. My father said his prayers. I helped Mother with the cooking.

I put the big pot on the stove. Mother takes a little flour, mixes it with water. She wants to make sweet noodles.

She asks Father what he wants to eat. He says he'll have the same as we do. Mother takes a smidgen of water and starts to knead the pastry. When she mixes the flour, her hand starts to give her trouble and she asks me to take over. She's in so much pain.

I come over to help her, but then she stops me. 'No, it's not worth it. Go and finish your schoolwork first or you'll end up doing badly tomorrow.'

99

So I go and do my homework. But in fact, I can't work. I watch Mother. Her hand hurts. But she has to cook now to prepare for the fast. She's such a kind and courageous woman. She treats her major illness like a minor one, even though she suffers from hideous stomach pains. She takes pleasure in helping others. To me, she's nobility itself.

Sunday 10 December.

This afternoon, Mother made a little food, a few vegetables, so that we could leave for Yuwang before sunset. If we don't make it back to school tonight, it will be serious. We won't be present for the first class tomorrow and the teacher will hit us. I ask Mother to heat up the vegetables quickly and to put the rolls in a bag.

But everything is already prepared. I haven't quite finished washing my hair and she finds time to help me.

Father and Mother decide to accompany us part of the way. When the moment comes to leave them, my throat tightens. Me, I'm working for my own future, but why are my parents taking so much trouble for us? Do they hope that their children's lives will be better than their own? Or is it simply that they want us to honour them. Sometimes I really can't understand them.

Monday 11 December.

After school today, my brother and I finish off our homework. I ask my aunt, Ma Shiping, if she'd like to come to the market with us.

'Yes, very much,' she says.

All three of us leave. In the street I meet my fifth uncle and ask him whether my father has come to town. Yes, he says. He's just bumped into him.

While my brother and I look for our father everywhere, we manage to lose Ma Shiping.

Fifth uncle has told us that Father came to buy vegetables to mark the end of the fast of Ramadan and we search high and low. Finally we find him. He still hasn't bought anything. I ask him why. He says he's waiting for the prices to go down, because the merchants prefer selling their products off at closing time rather than taking them back with them.

Father asks us what we'd like to eat.

'Nothing,' we answer in chorus.

None the less, he takes us to an apple stall, buys a few for us and recommends that we eat them with bread. Then he turns back to take the village road. He's got several hours of walking ahead of him.

Tuesday 12 December.

All the comrades say we're going to have a music test this afternoon. I'm suddenly frightened.

The music teacher comes in. The class head shouts, 'Everyone up.'

The teacher announces, 'Sit down. Exam time, today.'

My heart sinks ever lower. The teacher chooses Tian Yuzhou. He gets up and sings. Then, everyone has a turn, one after another. When my turn comes, the teacher asks me to get up.

'Sing.'

I start on 'Little Rooster Likes his Fight'.

'Very good!' she compliments me.

My heart immediately lifts. I'm full of joy. When I go home, I'll have a good grade to show my parents.

Wednesday 13 December.

This morning, after gym, it was time for natural sciences. The teacher came in and immediately said, 'Make good use of the fresh air this morning to recite off by heart lesson 25, "The First Snow".'

We all start to recite.

The teacher explains the text to us. I find him very engaging today. It's the first time all term that I've seen him smile and look relaxed. Yet, when he explains the text, I don't really understand his enthusiasm.

It's only during break that I realise what he meant. He was explaining what goes on in snowy regions. In the text, children play with snow, throw snowballs, make snowmen. I think the teacher must have been thinking of the pleasures of his own childhood. That's why he was so likeable today and there was a big smile on his face. Let's hope I've guessed correctly.

Thursday 14 December.

Our last class today is natural sciences. When the teacher has finished explaining the lesson, he says to us: 'What I'm teaching you today, I haven't taught to the two other classes.'

I don't believe him. Later I asked Li Mei, from class number two in the fifth year. She confirmed what he said.

Only then do I believe Teacher Chen's words. I must work hard not to disappoint his hopes of class number one of the fifth year.[45]

Saturday 16 December.

This morning, Father, Mother, my brothers and I are all sitting on the *kang* watching a series called 'Heroic Children'. Just as this first episode is drawing to an end, the second daughter of my second

---

45 Every year is made up of fast-track classes and slower ones for pupils with difficulties. Ma Yan is in class one, the top stream for her year.

uncle, Huahua, comes running in. She asks me, 'Little sister, do you want to go and watch a funeral?'

I ask my mother if I can go out. She agrees. I change my clothes and put on my shoes.

I go off with Huahua. We walk behind the coffin of an old village woman we barely know. We walk for a long time and I start to feel I have had enough. But since we've already come a long way, there's no point in turning back. When we get to the end of the procession, in the middle of the fields we hear the weeping of the dead woman's daughters and daughters-in-law. And I start crying, too, despite myself.

Monday 18 December.
Fine weather.

This morning, after gym, our Chinese teacher advised us to revise the first part of our book. 'There may very well be a test. Those who work well will be rewarded.'

Once again, my heart all but stopped beating. I was so anxious, I could barely get a word out.

The best pupils revise with a smile on their lips, confidence written on their faces. I and a few comrades, who are perhaps the worst in the class, watch the others study with fear in our hearts. I'm afraid I'm going to stay frozen like this, like the last time, because I have so little faith in myself.[46]

I lower my head. Then I remember that the teacher said that if we studied well, we would certainly do well in the test.

---

46 Ma Yan is a very good pupil and it's thanks to her results that she's got to where she is. Each time that her mother wanted to withdraw her from school for financial reasons, the teachers came to plead her case, explaining that she really should carry on. None the less, this appreciation is relative. The level of teaching in rural schools is well below that in the cities.

Tuesday 19 December.

After school, the comrades go out to get their meal. I stay behind in class all alone and write. Today, I'm fasting. There are only a few days left until the end of Ramadan and I want to hold out until the end.

When I go back to the dorm, the comrades are busy eating. They discuss things while they chew. I sit down beside them and listen.

Wednesday 20 December.

After classes, I go back to the dorm to sweep up. I have barely got through half of the room when the head of the dorm, Ma Jing, comes in and starts sweeping as well. I ask her why she's going to this trouble, and she replies that it's to help me.

When we've finished, we sit down on the bed to rest. Ma Xiaohong and my aunt come into the dorm. They're going to wash their hair, they announce. They boil a pot of water and get started. I go out on the porch to write in my diary, from where I can hear them talking. They criticise my attitude.

I feel like going in and telling them I can hear what they're saying. But since we've been friends for so many years, I don't.

Why is it that for some time now the people closest to me have been saying bad things about me? What is the answer to this mystery?

Saturday 23 December.

This afternoon, we have a history test. Our history teacher comes in holding the copies of the test. I haven't yet had time to read my course book and I'm very worried. I fear I'll fail. But when I learn we can use the book in the exam, I'm thrilled.

At this moment, I remember a little saying of Mother's and I decide not to open the book. I have to count on my true abilities in order to cross this hurdle.

After the exam, I check my answers against others'. I can hardly believe that mine are exactly the same as theirs.

You have to count on your own strengths truly to succeed.[47]

Tuesday 26 December.

This morning, Mother prepares dinner and cleans the house. She boils up a pot of water for me so that I can wash my clothes.[48] I pour the water into a tin basin and start my washing. I've only washed two things when a lot of people arrive, among them my grandmother. They talk and laugh so noisily that it feels as if the roof is going to fall in.

I carry on washing my school clothes, and think that it really is at home that things are happiest and that we forget our misfortunes.

Thursday 28 December.

This morning, Mother is ill. She has stomach pains and they make her suffer a great deal. I do all the housework for her. I cook some noodles for her too, and some yellow rice for the rest of us. After we've eaten, I wash out the pot. Then my brother and I go out to have fun.

---

47 An old Maoist saying has it that 'One has to rely on one's own strength'. The image is more applicable to the Revolution and the wars from which it stemmed than to education. But Ma Yan uses it for her own ends.

48 Ma Yan has only one set of clothes for school: a white shirt and red canvas trousers, an outfit that her mother bought for her at the end of the last school year so that she could take part in a ceremony celebrating Children's Day, when Ma Yan received a prize. She washes her clothes at home every weekend so that they're ready to wear on the Monday morning.

PART TWO

Ma Yan's diary starts again on 3 July 2001, after an interruption of six months during which it looked as if she might never return to school. During these six months, she carried on writing in her diary, but it went up in smoke . . . Her father had developed the habit of using his children's old notebooks for cigarette paper. Without knowing that's what he was doing, he had used his daughter's diaries.

At the beginning of July, Ma Yan was preparing to return to her village for the summer break, after having taken the entrance exam for the girls' senior school at Tongxin, the best school in her area.

Yesterday, I came back from Tongxin, the largest city in the district. It was the first time I'd been there. If it wasn't for this exam, I might never in my life have had the opportunity of going there and seeing the outside world.

Last night I slept next to my best friends, Ma Zhonghong and Ma Xiaohong. I woke up very early this morning to go to the market to find a tractor from my village. People assured me that a tractor had arrived, but I couldn't find it. So I sat down at the entrance to the market and waited for my father. The vehicle didn't come. Nor did my father. Tears in my eyes, I went back to school to get my bag. I looked for Teacher Chen so that he could open the dorm for me, but unfortunately he wasn't about. I had to get in through the window. I know it's a bad habit, but I had no choice.

By the time I found my bag, the tears were flowing all the way down to my clothes. Other children, too, are leaving for their holidays, but their parents are here to carry their things for them. I had to get my luggage out through the window, which is hard enough in itself.

On the street, the sun burns. It's hard to open my eyes. My back is running with sweat, as if it had been drenched with a bucket of water. I don't know whether it's because of the burning sun or because I'm carrying too much luggage.

At the market, I finally find a tractor from my village. I put all my things on it and go off once more to look for my father. I don't find him, but I bump into my third uncle. He asks me if I've eaten. When I say no, he invites me to have something to eat a little way further along the road. We come across two young women. Both of them suggest that we come into their restaurants. We go into one, and straight away, the other woman starts to swear at us.

The woman whose restaurant we're in asserts, pointing at me, 'This girl eats here often.'

I'm very surprised to hear that. This term, I've never eaten there. After the meal, I feel bad. Is it because she's poor that she has to lie like this? If her business was doing better, she wouldn't have to make up such stories.

Wednesday 4 July.

This afternoon, my mother and I go and visit the paternal grand-parents. When we arrive, my grandfather is sitting on the doorstep. He's watching over my fifth uncle's children. My grandparents live at this uncle's house.

We ask Grandpa where Grandmother is. He answers that she's in the big cave my uncle dug near his house. I run over there imagining that my grandmother is busy preparing a good meal. Once I'm inside, the first thing I see is her white hair, then her clothes, all soiled. She's turning the hay. I ask her what she's doing. She says the donkey has no food left and she's getting fodder for him.

I lower my head and wonder what use are we in this world. Those who have work can make a contribution towards the country. Those who don't only sleep and eat. My grandmother came into this world some eighty years ago. Why has she never known any happiness in her life? Did she annoy the heavens in some way? Or is her fate just a bad one . . .

Her mother died five months after she was born. She was raised by her maternal grandmother. Then she married my grandfather and led this difficult life.

Friday 13 July.
A fine day.

This afternoon, after cutting the wheat, my mother washed her hands and started making the bread we would take with us into the fields tomorrow.

My father is sitting on the threshold. He's rolling cigarettes. I'm off to wash my hair. My two brothers are spreading a plastic sheet outside because it's too hot to sleep indoors. We've been spending nights in the open air.

My mother finishes steaming the bread. She calls my father to the table. I come in after him. I take a bowl of black rice and swallow it down. The bowl empty, I want to get some more, but there's none left. My brother has eaten it all. I ask my mother whether I can have one of her rolls, but she says, 'No. It's for tomorrow.' She doesn't even let me nibble at a tiny one.

I go outside to sleep. I lie looking up at the stars and think: is it because I haven't passed the entrance exam for the girls' senior school that my mother is so angry with me? I begin to resent her. She won't even let me eat my fill before sleeping. My tears start to flow. But I also think she probably has her own reasons for being in a rage. Why does she take so much trouble over everything? It's always for our studies, so that we can succeed in life, have happy families of our own.

I have to work well. Even if I haven't got through the entrance exam this time,[49] in three years, I'll do it. I won't disappoint my parents.

---

49 Ma Yan has heard through rumour that she hasn't made it into the top girls' school in the district. She'll therefore go back to the school in Yuwang, which is of a lower calibre.

Saturday 14 July.
Good weather.

This afternoon, just after I've woken from my nap, someone comes to visit. It's the son of one of the village's rich men. His father is called Ma Zhanchuan. The villagers have given him the nickname of Lao Gan, or 'old prune' because he's so dry. His son has come to ask my father if we could cut their wheat for them.[50] My father goes to see them. On his return, I ask him whether we've accepted the work. 'Yes,' he says.

The whole family goes off to the fields to harvest Ma Zhanchuan's wheat. They pretend they only have thirteen mu, but in my opinion there are at least sixteen. While we're working, my mother stands tall and says to us: 'When we've cut the wheat, I'll give you each ten yuan. You can eat whatever you want at the market.'

I literally jump for joy, then I suddenly notice a comrade who passed the entrance exam for the school in Tongxin. My heart sinks down to my knees. I can't take my eyes off the girl. But nor can I see straight. It seems to me the hills and the sky are moving. Mother looks at me and asks what's wrong.

'Nothing,' I tell her. 'Nothing.'

I bend down again. What earthly right do I have to buy good things at the market? I haven't even managed to get into a good senior school. I should be ashamed. I shall have to work really hard not to fail at the next try and disappoint my parents.

Sunday 15 July.
Fine weather.

This afternoon, at four o'clock, after our siesta, Mother started to prepare dinner. I helped her to make the fire. After we'd eaten, the

50 Poor peasants, like Ma Yan's family, hire themselves out to richer ones with more land during harvest time.

whole family went back to the fields on the plain to cut more wheat. A little while after that, my mother was tying the wheat into bales when she suddenly sat down and went very pale. She moaned softly and said her stomach pains had begun again.

There she is, sitting in the wheat, but we carry on mowing with our sickles.

Tears and the perspiration of pain run down my mother's face. Her eyes are red. Her hands are arched over her stomach. My father tells her to go home. No, she'll wait for us, she says. I lower my head and think, Why does my mother want to do this harvesting when she is so gravely ill? Why?

For us, of course. So that we don't have to lead a life like hers.

And what have I done for her in return? I haven't even been able to bring home the honour of succeeding in my entrance exam.

The whole family working in the fields.

Monday 16 July.
Fine weather.

This morning while we were scything the wheat in the fields, my legs suddenly began to ache horribly. I sat down for a moment.

My mother started straight in on me. 'Really, Ma Yan. You're exaggerating!'

My little brother, Ma Yiting, rubs it in. 'Those who study, all exaggerate. Look at our other comrade over there. It takes her half an hour just to get up!'

And my mother adds: 'Even if the girl's exaggerating, she's brought honour on her family. She's succeeded in her exam. You . . . you disappoint me too much.'

At that moment, tears I'm not even aware of start pouring down my cheeks. They won't stop. My mother is always extreme in her comments. She says things, then repeats them, then insists on them. How to bear it all?

I mustn't resent her. At heart, I'm only angry at myself. If I had got into the girls' school, she wouldn't have spoken such hurtful words. She has her own problems. If she works hard, it's so that we can go to school.

In the village, I'm good at a great many things and few of the children can do better than me. That's why my mother counted on my getting into the best school. But I let her down. How could she not be disappointed in me? She must be very upset.

Saturday 28 July.
A fine day.

This afternoon, around three o'clock, my mother is so ill, she can't even get up. My brother and I give her some medicine to ease her pain. We rub her stomach with a cream.[51] We haven't finished

---

51 An unguent used in traditional Chinese medicine.

114

when my second cousin, Ma Yiwu, the son of my father's eldest brother, arrives.

This youth of twenty-five has completed a degree from a technical school, but he's having trouble finding work. He says that work in a successful business is bought with bribes and corruption.

He comes in and sits down at the edge of the bed. He looks bothered. My mother asks him if he's found work. My cousin answers:

'It's easy to find work, but you have to pay for it under the table. If I had two thousand yuan, I could get into an enterprise. The problem is money. My family has no money. In a few days I'm going off and will get any old job. When I've earned enough money, then I'll buy myself into a proper position.'

I'm sitting on the stool and I notice that his eyes have filled with tears. When I see his hair, already going white, and his tortured face, my heart breaks. Why is it that the children of two generations of soldiers can't find work? Today, the grandson of a military hero has a degree, but no money, and as a result can't find a job. Are the heavens blind? Do they only know how to take care of the most wicked people? Are they mocking the lives and deaths of good people? It's all so unjust.

I don't know where my second cousin went off to. I hope he'll find a good job soon.[52] It will make me incredibly happy for him.

Sunday 29 July.
A fine day.

After lunch today, Mother called me by my second name. 'Haha, get a bag. Go and cut some grass for the donkey.'

I went out on my own. The sun was burning and attacked me

---

52 Since writing this, Ma Yan's cousin has moved to Yinchuan, the capital of the autonomous region of Ningxia, and has found modest employment.

with its heat.[53] I don't know when I annoyed the heavens enough for them to punish me in such a manner. My face is scorched.

Climbing the hillside, I can't even keep my eyes open. Is Mother trying to punish me by sending me out here, alone in the midday heat, to cut grass for the donkey.

We've had drought for years and there isn't much grass up on the hill. I pick up the scythe, but even as I cut the dry grass, I can't prevent the tears running down my face. Mother is punishing me. If I had got into the girls' school, she would have asked my two brothers to help me. My failure means I'm the only one to suffer.

But what does my suffering and exhaustion matter? I have to pursue my ideal with courage and persistence, come what may. Though I don't know if I'll ever reach my distant goal.

Monday 30 July.
A fair day.

This afternoon, when I want to start writing my diary, I can't find my pen. I ask my brothers. No, they haven't seen it. I look for it in the place where I was doing my writing yesterday and it isn't there either. I ask my mother. She says that yesterday she noticed that I had left my pen and notebook on the bed and she was worried that they'd get lost, so she put them away in the drawer. But my pen isn't there. I'm distraught.

---

53 Summer temperatures in China can go up to 40 degrees centigrade, even through a leaden sky. This has been particularly the case in these last few years of drought in the north of the country, and especially in the region of Ningxia. There was a respite in 2002 when all of China had exceptionally heavy rainfall. In the south, this sadly led to catastrophic floods which killed over 1,000 people. In Ningxia and other parts of the north and north-west, the abundant rain meant the best harvests in twenty years. In July of 2002 Zhangjiashu wore exceptionally bright colours.

You're probably going to start laughing. 'A pen. What a minor thing to get so distressed about!'

If only you knew the trouble I had to take to get that pen. I saved up my pocket money for two weeks. Some of my comrades have two or three pens, but I had none and I couldn't resist buying one.

The difficulties I confronted in getting this pen are a mirror of all my other problems. My mother had given me some money with which to buy bread. For days, I had only eaten yellow rice. I preferred going hungry and economising so that I could buy the pen. How I suffered for that pen!

Then I got another pen. I won it at the Children's Day celebrations on the 1st of June for being a good student. From then on, I no longer lacked pens.

But my dear old pen gave me a sense of power. It made me understand the meaning of a difficult life or a happy life. Every time I see the pen, it's as if I were seeing my mother. It's as if she was encouraging me to work hard and make it into the girls' senior school.

Now I've disappointed my mother. What am I but a useless burden? At school, I lead a life which isn't worth while. I couldn't make it into the girls' school. What's the use of going on?

But I must think positively. I have to succeed. I will, I really will find an ideal job. And I'll be happy with it.

Saturday 4 August.
A fine day.

This morning, Mother and Father went off to work in the fields. No one had yet taken them any bread. My brother, Ma Yichao, said he would go and asked me to cut the grass for the donkey. I took the basket and the scythe and went out. I walked along to my fourth uncle's house and called my other brother, Ma Yiting, who was there and we went off together. A few small children followed us. We all worked side by side. We each cut a bagful of grass, then went home laughing and chatting. Everyone looked very happy.

Maybe they think this is the end of their work for the day, that now it's their turn to ask for things . . . Will they go on living in this ridiculous manner?

I must study hard. When I'm older I'll make sure that my children have happy days, that they're not always caught up in money problems, which is the case at home now. If they don't go to school, I'll ask them to grow grass and tend the ox and the sheep. Then what they earn in a year will be enough to keep them.

But I'm already planning my future life even though I have no idea if I'll be able to succeed. Let's hope so.

Sunday 5 August.
A fine day.

This afternoon, when my parents got back from their work in the fields, they fell asleep on the bed. I went out to tether the donkey and give him some grass to eat. When I came back inside, I saw that my parents were even more deeply asleep. I didn't wake them. I found a little wood for burning and some dung and brought them in. I took yesterday's ashes out of the stove and started to light the fire. But it wouldn't take. Nothing I did would make it light. I wanted to die.

At that moment, I understood how painstaking Mother has to be when she prepares our food. Just getting the fire going is a struggle. I've tried it just once and it makes me want to die. How has Mother managed to keep the fire alight, let alone do all our cooking for so long?

I started helping in the kitchen at the age of seven. Many years have passed since then. I've also lit the fire in the stove on occasion, but always with the help of my brothers. Today I'm alone. But I've got to get it going.

Finally, I manage and I can start the cooking. When the food is ready I wake my parents, so they can eat. During the meal, Mother starts to tell stories from her childhood. It's so nice to listen to her. She laughs and her eyes seem to laugh at the same time. I want her to laugh all the time and wish she had no more worries to confront and reasons to be sad.

If only my wish would come true!

On the *kang*, the great cement bed: one of the rare moments in which the family is happy and reunited.

Thursday 9 August.
A fair day.

This morning my two brothers went out to cut grass for the donkey while Father was working on the threshing floor. Mother is ill. She stayed in bed.

I tried to get the fire going for the meal, but my brothers came back before it had taken. I asked them why they had been so quick.

'We want to work today. When we've finished eating, sister She, a friend from the village, is coming to pick us up so that we can walk to Wangshanwa together and help with the harvest there. It's an hour away.'

Soon lunch is ready. Sister She arrives. I fill two bowls for my parents and also offer one to sister She. But she doesn't want to eat. So I offer the bowl to my brother. We're sitting on the threshing floor which has been tidied up and we laugh and talk. Sister She tells us a story.

'When we go to pick *fa cai*, we always have a great time. My fifth uncle's grandmother always sings while she's scything. And she dances. All the people at the top of the hill stop working and just watch her. She's such a spectacle. She may be old, they say, but she's got a joyous heart and an attractive character.'

I don't believe this explanation of the grandmother's character. I believe this woman to be sad and unhappy. How do I know? Because my mother's done the same work. So this grandmother who's been cutting grass all her life into her old age, who's never had a decent outfit of clothes, who had to earn money to find a good wife for her son . . . well, now her life is so unenviable that her only joy is dancing. If she doesn't dance now, she'll never have time to dance at all.

Why are we alive? The rich die after having known all kinds of pleasures. It's a happy death. The poor live with tears in their eyes. When they die, their death is painful. And that's the truth of it.

As with many of China's peasants, work on the land is not enough to feed the inhabitants of the Xi Hai Gu triangle. *Fa cai* was a play on words which the poorer peasants enjoyed before it plunged them into illegalities.

The two characters of *fa cai*, which depict a hairy grass that grows wild on the steppes of north-west China, also mean 'to make one's fortune'. 'Get rich' is the greeting the Chinese use at the lunar New Year. Both the Cantonese and the inhabitants of Hong Kong were seduced by the pun on fortune that the vegetable grass provided. In the 1990s they started to eat it in great quantities in salad or soup, thereby making the fortune of the peasants of the north-west. Despite its lack of any particular taste or nutriment, the price of this grass from the arid steppes soared.

This passion of the southern Chinese, born of superstition, enabled hundreds of thousands of peasants to survive by harvesting *fa cai*. Ma Yan's family are among them.

The harvesting of *fa cai* was, however, outlawed by the government in 2000 for environmental reasons. According to the Beijing experts, over 130,000 square kilometres of Inner Mongolia alone were turned into desert by the pulling up of *fa cai*. It's thought to be one of the causes of the violent sandstorms which hit Beijing each spring and travel as far as Korea and Japan.

An American report of 1998 confirms this: 'Human activity, not climatic change, seems to be the principal cause of desertification in Inner Mongolia . . . Two hundred thousand impoverished peasants, largely from the

Hui minority in the autonomous region of Ningxia, are responsible for the devastation of the pastures of Inner Mongolia.'

The prohibition on harvesting *fa cai* is probably grounded in good sense, but it none the less threatens to plunge the poorest peasants, who have no other means of subsistence, into total misery. We came across some of them near the town of Tongxin. Twenty peasants were crowded on to the trailer tied to the back of a rudimentary tractor. They were sitting on their sacks and bales of *fa cai*, their faces covered to protect them from the wind and the sand. With a jolting slowness, they were going back to their mountain villages in the south of the province with their precious cargo.

Fa cai is a dry black grass, a little like algae, but as fine as hair. For them it's like gold dust. They had travelled a distance of four hundred kilometres to pick this 'caviar of the steppes' on the borders of Ningxia and Inner Mongolia, taking with them a small supply of food and water. Most of these peasants were very young, but among them were a few old women and two men. Picking *fa cai* has long been their main activity: some of them have been harvesting it for twenty years.

The prohibition, which went into force on 1 August 2000, hasn't stopped them. 'Even if we're frightened, we have no choice. We have nothing to eat,' explain the women who have come from the drought belt. 'At home, we have no electricity and no water. Nothing grows. I have to sell this *fa cai* to feed my children,' says the oldest of the women, whose face is lined with misery.

For this arduous and illegal work, the peasants hope to earn about 60 to 70 yuan, once the costs of food and transport of 25 yuan each have been deducted. This is a derisory sum in today's China, but it's hardly inconsiderable for peasants whose annual income never exceeds a few hundred yuan.

Some of them only go home for a week or two before leaving again for the north. There is a lot of *fa cai* to cut. The risks of being stopped by the police are rather less severe than those of being attacked by angry Mongolian herdsmen, furious at the plight of their disappearing pastures. The American report of 1998 led to battles between the Mongolians and the Hui, which the police were incapable of stopping. (The police's petrol allowance for an entire month could be spent in a matter of days in pursuit of these groups.)

The peasants used to sell their harvest in the large urban markets like Tongxin. Some four thousand people made their way there regularly and the *fa cai* trade became

On the roads of Ningxia: the trailer of a tractor, bringing back the exhausted women who have been picking *fa cai*.

the primary activity of the town; it also had a factory for treating the grass in which three hundred workers were employed. In a neighbouring commune, a local official confided to us that 70 per cent of the population were engaged in activities related to the harvesting of *fa cai*, which made up a third of the local revenue. There isn't a single family that hasn't a *fa cai* story to tell. Ma Yan's diary shows us what a crucial role the grass plays in the economy of the region.

Officially, all this stopped in 2000, though no alternative source of income was suggested to make up for the substantial fall in peasant earnings.

Thus a clandestine trade has now come into being. Intermediaries from the south of China go from village to village buying the *fa cai* from the peasants. The prices have fallen because there's less room for negotiation this way than on the open market. The middlemen make the biggest profit: the price is three or four times higher when they resell than when they buy. By the time the *fa cai* reaches Hong Kong's fashionable restaurants, the soup from which it is made can cost up to $500 HK (or about £5.60) a portion. On an Internet site for the Chinese diaspora, dedicated to 'culinary symbolism', you can even find a recipe for a much-sought-after dish – dried oysters *fa cai*, described as 'a happy event which brings good fortune'.

In fact, the local authorities in this poorest of Chinese regions seem sensitive to the fate of the peasants and show little desire to follow the diktat which has come from the distant capital. The sheer number of tractors tugging their loads of women and sacks filled with *fa cai* that we came cross in broad daylight on the roads of Ningxia points to the lack of enforcement of the prohibition.

'We have to apply the directives which come from Beijing; but we also have to think of the general welfare of the people,' says a local Communist official without much conviction. His village is one of the few which recommends its unemployed inhabitants to find other kinds of work.

An official stops a woman who's telling us she has just come back from picking *fa cai* and recommends that she says she is returning from a trip. Here, too, it's important not to lose face.

In all the neighbouring houses, the peasants confirm that, despite everything, they're still picking the hairy grass. 'If the police stop us, they take our harvest and beat us,' says a young girl. But like her neighbours, that will hardly stop her going back to the steppes in the north. For all of them, *fa cai* doesn't mean getting rich, it simply means 'survival'.

'Everyone here makes their living from *fa cai*,' another woman tells us. By way of explanation she gestures towards the fields they have so laboriously planted and tended, but in which nothing grows because of the lack of rain.

Saturday 11 August.
A fine day.

Today at midday I finished eating, then went into the kitchen to wash the pot. My parents and brothers stayed in the room to watch a film on television. I washed up then came back in to write my diary.

Mother is feeling very bad. Always these stomach pains. I write a few words on a scrap of paper that I stick to the door: 'Mother is ill. She's resting. Don't go in unless it's urgent. Come back later.'

I haven't quite finished writing this, when Mother calls me. She's feeling sick, nauseous. The traditional medicine hasn't helped at all. I come close to her and she takes my hand and won't let it go. She's still feeling awful. I call Father to come and have a look at her, but he only chides her. Mother cries and laughs at the same time.

I'm terrified. I don't know why Mother has had so many bizarre illnesses these last years. When she's going through a crisis, the whole family is desperate. The worst thing is that when she's ill, the sweat pours down her face like water. I don't know how she can stand it. In her shoes, I think I'd have died of the pain. I really hope she gets better soon.

Sunday 12 August.
Fine weather.

Tomorrow I have to travel a long distance to harvest *fa cai*. I'm following the road my mother has taken so many times. Now that she's ill, I have to go with my father and my brother, so that we can earn enough to live. And take care of Mother. Then I want to earn a little more money so that I can make my dreams come true. I want to go and study in the district school. But since Mother has been ill, our lives are so hard.

I really don't know why the heavens are treating us like this. Why everything is so unjust.

Monday 27 August.

Tonight, I'm just repairing a wooden box when Mother asks my brother and me to go out and cut a little grass from behind the house for the donkey, who hasn't eaten all day. We go. My brother has only torn off a single handful of grass when he stops to pee.

Ten minutes go by and he still isn't back. I call him and he appears, grumbling, 'I can't pull it up. I'll have to go and get a scythe.' Again he runs off and I have time to cut almost a bagful of grass.

I call him again, loudly. This time he comes back with a little grass and has the gall to ask me why I'm not cutting any more. I tell him I've finished and it's his turn now.

At home, Mother starts snapping at me again. 'How long do you expect me to continue being your servant? Since you've come home, you behave like a mandarin.' I don't know what she means by the word mandarin.[54]

She adds, 'You're like my mother, or my grandmother. I serve you. I've raised you. Do you think you have worked as hard? I'm ashamed of you. The daughter of the Yangs is younger than you, yet she passed the entrance exam for the girls' school. And you? You've disappointed me far too much. Tear up all your books. There's no point in going to school tomorrow. You and your ancestors . . . who are you, after all? Your ancestors begged in order to eat. Even if I finance your studies, what will you be able to do? It would be better if you died right away. Every day, I hope that you're going to die. If you die, I'll bury you under a bit of earth and at least I'll be at peace for a few days.'

---

54 The mandarins were the highest ranking of Chinese civil servants and always came from the most cultivated sectors of society.

I'm staggered. I don't know why Mother is talking like this. Is she in a rage or does she really believe what she's saying?

In any case, she's wrong. Why doesn't she put herself in my place? Tomorrow I have to leave. And what do I feel? It's hard leaving my family, leaving my mother. My heart isn't light. And when Mother speaks to me like this, tears flood my heart. I can't contradict her. I have to win all the honours, both for my mother and for my ancestors. I want them to be at peace and proud of me, even if they're in the ground.

The origins of Ma Yan's family are a sore point, a sad and sensitive one which rears up at moments of tension. Apart from the sufferings which his origins led to, Ma Yan's paternal grandfather Ma Shunji, this beggar's son who was sold to a local landowner, had a difficult time when he came back to the village after all his years in Korea. There was no work. The war veteran had a lot of trouble adjusting to life outside the military.

There is great secrecy in the family regarding the subject of Ma Shunji's return to civilian life and the failures which rebounded on the head of Ma Yan's father, Ma Dongji. His infamous parentage, which put him at the bottom of the social hierarchy in this traditional rural village, compounded with his economic failure, make him an ideal scapegoat. Even his wife treats him as one in moments of anger.

According to Bai Juhua, because he couldn't read her husband allowed himself to be cheated at the start of the 1980s when the collectives came to an end and land was reallocated. He was granted less land than he should have been. Today, Ma Yan's father, although he's a veteran and proud of having served his country, has only got eight mu.

A local official tells a different story. When the lands were divided up, Ma Dongji was still a bachelor and thus only entitled to eight mu.

Eventually five people had to live off this small piece of land. The situation is inescapable, the fruit of history. With so little land, and ancient agricultural techniques compounded by years of drought, Ma Yan's family has little hope of seeing an improvement in its situation.

Tuesday 28 August.
A cloudy day.

This morning at about six o'clock, my father got the cart and donkey ready. He took my brother, Ma Yichao, and me to Yuwang. School is about to start. It's our first year in the senior school.

When we get there, Father helps take our things out of the cart, then sets off for home. We're alone again.

The bell announces the beginning of classes. I'm in a different one from Ma Yichao, so he heads off in one direction, I in another.

When I get there, the teacher asks me why I'm in class four.

I say, 'Maybe it's because I didn't work well enough.'

'Why do you say that? This year is different from last, when the best students were in classes one, two and three. This year the classes aren't streamed according to your level. I hope you're not getting discouraged.'

I take in what the teacher says and store it up inside me.

Having told me to sit down, he's gone out of the room.

The comrades are making a lot of noise, like mice fighting once the cat has left. My head feels completely empty, except for the noise around me. These boys and girls are all a little bigger than me. They swear all the time and they don't look like senior school students. Our class has seventy in it. Imagine what it's like when everyone speaks at the same time. How is one to work in here!

I'm so upset. What I hate most about myself is the fact that I cry so easily. I don't want to cry now, but I can't seem to stop myself.

The senior school in Yuwang has over 1,000 pupils. It consists of a series of enormous red-brick buildings, each of which contains overcrowded classrooms, devoid of essential equipment. The benches are makeshift. There is a single blackboard. Plaster peels from walls unpainted for years. There are no teaching aids of any kind and just one rudimentary sports field.

The only recent innovation, seen when we last returned, is a gift from Chinese emigrants to Hong Kong: a large satellite dish which permits access to teaching by television, notably better than that available here and a means of raising standards. In a school such as this, the task of the teachers is formidable, and that of the students almost impossible. How many of these will have the opportunity of taking their studies further and getting to university? Like Ma Yan, so many of them desire just that.

Ma Yan invites us to visit her 'kingdom', which is what she calls her dormitory. There are sixteen girls here, all of them from the villages roundabout, which they return to at weekends. The beds are crowded against each other, but the girls don't complain.

Just as in the last school, one of the school buildings is a kitchen where they go to fetch their meals, and bring them back to the dormitory to eat on their beds.

Wednesday 29 August.
A fine day.

After school I meet two comrades who were in my class in the primary. They haven't gone home because we have a study period in the evenings and their families live far away. Their results are a little worse than mine, one or two points lower. But they're in classes one or two. As for me, I'm in class four. I'm too depressed to talk to them.

Other friends come and play. They look happy. I think of my two best friends from primary. But they've left school now. I'm all alone. Their families are better off than mine, but they don't want to go to school any more. I don't understand them.

The study hour arrives. The English teacher asks me to go to class three. The teacher there tells me I'm in his group. I find all this very strange.

Ma Yan's senior school, like all schools,
teaches political and civic values.

This afternoon my old primary-school friends, Ma Shaolian and Bai Xue, come to my dorm. They're not boarders. I'm very happy to see them again: it's as if we were back in primary school. They look as pretty and happy as ever.

We sit down to talk. Without knowing why, I turn my head to the right. I see a comrade taking a school book down and starting to read. My friends say, 'What on earth is she studying now? All the teachers are fond of her.'

I think to myself, Here's this girl who's already a good student, but she carries on working while I sit around doing nothing at all. That can't be right.

I say goodbye to my friends and go back to my books. I really have to work hard so that I can eventually get that ideal job and have Mother stop worrying about me.

Ma Yan and her comrades in the dormitory.

133

Tuesday 4 September.
A fine day.

In the last class today, there's a general clean-up of the school.

The term is starting. All the comrades are happy. We've finally arrived at the portal of secondary education. We have a lot of enthusiasm, a lot of goodwill. We put a lot of energy into our work.

Our teacher asks us to clean the area behind the school. He's like an old hen taking a group of chicks off to feed. The comrades make clucking sounds and clean with vigour. In very little time, the work is done. The teacher tells us to go off and rest.

All the comrades have gone and I'm standing alone on the sports field, watching the others at work. This school must have 1,000 pupils. They work hard. If there were more like them, we'd certainly be able to plant more trees for China.[55] How wonderful it would be if there were more of us.

Thursday 6 September.
A fine day.

Today after school, some parents came to collect their children. They went off together to eat good things in the market. My brother and I haven't eaten for two days. We only have hard old black bread to chew at. So we go off to market to look for our parents. But they haven't come. I think that Mother is probably not at home. When we left last week, she said she was going to go off and pick *fa cai* on Monday or Tuesday.

I think so often of Mother! I don't know how long it will be until I see her again. I want to see her hands, her poor hands.

---

55 In order to combat desertification, the government launched a reforestation pro-gramme. For each mu of farmable land on which trees are planted, a peasant receives a cereal subsidy for seven years.

Friday 7 September.
A dull day.

This morning, our last lesson is politics.[56] A very tall teacher comes in. He's about twenty-seven and exceedingly handsome. He must be a Han, while all my other teachers are Hui. Their pronunciation is very different from that of Huis, very rigid. We don't understand everything they say. I only grasped a single whole phrase: 'Make progress in your studies.'

Why do all the teachers repeat this? It makes us feel we're under constant pressure. But I'm going to do my best. I'll achieve my goals.

Saturday 8 September.
A lovely day.

After school, a few of the comrades with money were allowed to leave early. They got on to a tractor for a yuan. Only my little brother and I are walking. On the track, the sun burns down on us and we think we'll die of thirst. My brother asks an old man for a watermelon. We both crouch at the side of the road and eat, like dogs who've been chased out of the house. We really look pitiful.

When we get home, the yard is empty. I know Mother has gone. My paternal grandfather comes out of the house and says, 'Ah, my little grandchildren are home. Come, you must be very hungry.'

My brother says that there's a watermelon in the wooden school box. I cut it and share it with my grandfather. While I eat, I think

56 This is a little like a class in citizenship or current affairs, but inspired by Communist ideology. Students are taught patriotism, the cult of the Party Heroes, the need to reintegrate Taiwan into China, but also 'how to be civilised and polite', hygiene, and so on.

of my mother. I don't even know how she is.[57] Her stomach was bad again. And the picking is such hard work. Really hard. Especially if you're ill.

When will I be able to stop Mother exhausting herself for us like this? I really want her to have a better life. One in which she doesn't have to go so far away to work. One in which she won't suffer. I just hope my wish comes true.

Sunday 9 September.
A sombre day.

This afternoon, my paternal grandmother came to visit. It's as if my mother had come home. I gave her a slice of watermelon. I was writing my diary at the table.

While she eats, my grandmother says to me: 'You look so serious! I really wonder what it is you're writing. Our lives have so little interest.'

'Don't say that, Grandmother,' I reply. 'I'll read you what I'm writing.'

While I read, tears flow down my grandmother's face.

'We old ones,' she says to me, 'we're good for nothing. And it's because of us that you suffer.'

'Oh no, Grandmother. Don't talk like that. It's because of you that I've been able to live until now. Without you, I wouldn't have understood anything about life.'

I think, then, of some things my mother keeps repeating. 'No matter all our problems and exhaustion, I'm going to pay for your studies so that you become people of talent, so that you make a

---

57 Ma Yan's mother has gone off, as she often has to do, for at least two weeks to harvest *fa cai* in Inner Mongolia. She should earn about 100 yuan, an indispensable sum in the family's meagre finances.

contribution to the country, so that you don't live a life like mine, which has no interest or value in it.'

I won't disappoint my mother. She'll see what kind of daughter she has.

It's market day again, today. I have to go back to school, this school that I can't leave. But since today is Teachers' Day we're on holiday.

When I get down from the tractor, the driver asks me for money. But I haven't any. I tell him I'll pay him the next time. But he won't let me go. I take out my pen and offer it to him. He refuses. This time, it's he who says I can pay him on the next journey.

When I go through the school gates, I'm crying without knowing why. Maybe because I'm thinking of Mother. I don't know how she's getting on up in the mountains, but I know how tough life is there.

Every time I'm faced with a difficulty, I think of my mother.

What I told the driver was a lie. The teachers say students shouldn't lie. They should be honest. But I had no choice. I asked my father for money and he told me we had no money: don't I know the problems the family is facing?

I stopped asking him for money then. If I had gone on, he would have got into a rage.

Had I explained all that to the driver, he would have made fun of me, and especially of my father. He would have condemned him and thought, What a father, a good for nothing. He can't even pay for a tractor ride for his child!

My father does his best. And I don't want anyone saying bad things about him. That's why I lied.

137

Wednesday 12 September.
A fine day.

This evening during study time, the English teacher comes in, mounts the platform and asks, 'Do you really want to learn English?'

We shout a unanimous, 'Yes.'

He goes on, 'Since you really want to learn English well, I suggest you each contribute one yuan and we'll be able to buy a tape recorder so that you can work on your own during study hours in the evening. How about it?'

The comrades agree.

The teacher goes on. 'Do any of you have financial problems?'

'No,' they all reply in chorus.

He adds, 'If anyone has a money problem, put your hand up.'

I put my hand up.

The teacher asks, 'Does your family have problems?'

I answer him in English, 'Yes.'

Since he's the English teacher, I'm meant to speak to him in English.

He says, 'If you really have financial problems, you won't have to contribute. Some families are in real difficulty. They can't even pay their children's school fees.'

I think of my third year of primary school. I had no money with which to buy school books. Mother and a few women she knows went off to pick *fa cai*. With that money, I could buy my own books. But I missed a few months of school. At the beginning, I understood nothing at all. Then, after two or three months of hard work, I caught up.

I feel like shouting at the top of my lungs: My mother is excessively kind to her children. There is nothing she won't do for them. Instead I will write it down. 'Mother, you are great. I love you. I love your spirit. You are so strong. So pure. You're an example to your daughter. In your daughter's heart you will always be a great woman.'

Thursday 13 September.
A fine day.

This evening, during study hours, I look up and notice that I'm all alone in the room. It looks bigger than usual. Suddenly I'm frightened. I grab my rucksack and fly from the room like a gust of wind.

Outside I meet my friend Yang Yuehua from class four. She's walking very slowly. It seems strange. Usually she's so open and friendly. What's wrong with her today? I ask her what's going on.

It seems, her test went very badly. She cries and I console her. 'It's only a small test. You'll have lots of opportunity to do better . . .'

She replies through her tears, 'My mother has worked so hard for me. And this is the way I pay her back. I can't even thank her properly for all those rolls she makes for me every week.'

I'm full of admiration for her. She has clear ideas. Surely she'll be able to study well and have a good career.

Friday 14 September.
A grey day.

This morning, after classes, I went to get a bowl of rice. My comrade, Ma Yongmei, went to get water. When we had finished the rice, I put my hand into the very back of the wooden bread box which I keep on my bed, but the bread had all gone long ago. I'm still hungry, because between the two of us, we've only had a half-pound of rice.

You're probably going to say, half a pound for two, isn't that enough? But a half-pound only fills a small bowl. We shared it. Each of us was only allowed half. If you think that fills us up . . . On top of it, we've run out of rolls.

I watch the others who are eating watermelon, my mouth starts to water despite myself. I've had a cold for a few days and I feel quite sick. I sit dumbly on the edge of my bed. A comrade sees my state and gives me a pill. I feel better after that. That pill is more precious to me than treasure. This girl is called Bai Jing and her image is now engraved on my soul. She's someone one can take as a model.

Saturday 15 September.
A grey day.

Today is the beginning of the weekend. My brother and I walk along our interminable track. From the road, we can see fields full of melons. We're very hungry. My brother goes off into the fields to steal a little onion, a few turnips, and we eat them on our way. I know that stealing is wrong and that students shouldn't do such things. But what are we to do? If we don't steal from the fields of others, we probably won't make it home.

I walk slowly. My legs are very painful. I think I'm the unhappiest girl in the whole world.

I think of my mother again. I don't know how she is. She gets up at five-thirty in the morning and works till seven in the evening. Every day she and the other women who have gone to pick the *fa cai* walk with their eyes on the ground, their backs bent to the sky. How many mountains has she scaled this way?

Mother is the saddest and most unfortunate mother in the world. I have to carry on working hard so that she can have a better time in the second half of her life. So that she can finally take things easier.

Sunday 16 September.
A little rain.

Today I have to go back to school. Father has got our things ready for us and given us enough money to get a tractor ride to Yuwang. We climb up on the back wagon. A little further on, the granddaughter of the third paternal grandfather[58] joins us. My second uncle then climbs up on the tractor. He puts his niece on his lap, and fearing that she may get cold, he wraps a bag over her legs. She's already thirteen. Doesn't she know how to take care of herself?

I see them laugh. I also see my little brother shivering from cold. I give him my hat. On this rainy morning, my anger reaches boiling point.

My paternal grandfather was adopted. He's not really close to these people, who look down on him. My mother won't tolerate any contempt for our generation. She wants us to become people of substance. The trouble my parents take on our account is enormous. When I see the looks of these people, I think of my grandfather. It's for him that we need to study, so that people look up to us for the rest of our lives.

Monday 17 September.
Rain.

Last night, during the study hour, we had an English test. I found it easy. In less than half an hour, I'd finished. The teacher in charge asked us to give him our papers when we had finished. He lectured me, 'At that speed, how can you possibly have done well?'

I gave him my paper none the less.

But this morning the comrades are all abuzz. They're all saying, 'Ma Yan may work well, but she didn't come top of the class!'

As I listen to them, I'm ashamed. My parents have done so much for me and this is the way I repay them.

Then I reminded myself that there were more exams to come, at half-term and at the end of term. By then, I'll have made great progress. I'll work really hard, with no slacking. I just hope my wishes come true.

58 This is one of Ma Shunji's brothers from the family who adopted him.

Tuesday 18 September.
Rain.

When our last class is over, our English teacher asks us to stay for another twenty minutes to copy out words. After that, we go and get our food, but there's nothing left. There are a few teachers in the canteen, too, so I deliberately protest in a loud voice.

'Our stomachs are crying out with hunger. We've run here as quickly as we could, and there's nothing left. We pupils, we dream of nothing but these two bowls of rice from morning until evening. How do you expect us to make it through the day? If there were some bread at least . . . But there's no bread. And on top of it all, it's a rainy day! Our spirits grow weaker and weaker, especially on empty stomachs.'

The teachers say nothing. How I want to go home and eat my fill. I'll come back to school only when my stomach's full.

Then I remind myself that to study well, you probably have to put up with some suffering.

Thursday 20 September.
A grey day.

At noon, I came back from the canteen with some rice. I put the bowl on the bed. Ma Yongmei divided the rice in two and took her share. Before I could start on my bowl, my little brother Ma Yichao arrives. He asks, 'Sister, have you still got tickets for the canteen? I want to buy some rice.'

I borrow a ticket and give it to him.

Then he asks me if I've eaten.

'Yes, I have.'

But he guesses that it isn't true.

'You haven't eaten. Your lips are dry. The lips of people who have eaten are moist.'

142

A little while later he comes back and returns the canteen ticket. He says there's no more rice. He goes off again.

How can I help him? I have no money, no bread. I don't know what to do . . . Yet I'm his older sister and if I have no sense of responsibility, what am I good for? I cry. I tell myself it's not altogether my fault that our family's financial situation is so dire.

It's impossible to describe the sensation of HUNGER.

Sunday 30 September.
A bright day.

This afternoon we come back from the cornfields and I'm so hungry, I think I can see smoke coming out of my stomach. As soon as Mother arrives, she goes to the kitchen to prepare food. I ask my father for a yuan so that I can buy an English notebook. One of my cousins, the son of my fourth uncle, comes to visit. He tells me that my mother has lent my fourth-grade books to other children in the primary school. I ask her if this is true and she confirms it.

I'm angry because these books are still useful to me. How could she have given them away so easily? I want to be able to revise. There are questions I still don't understand.

For some time now, when the teacher is lecturing, I haven't been seeing clearly. He'll say for example that this is an even and this an odd number, but I can't clearly distinguish what he's writing on the blackboard. Nor can I hear properly. I have to attend closely to what the teachers and pupils are saying. When you're shortsighted, it's hard to follow the work. If you don't see properly you can only count on your ears. And when your ears are also bad, then . . .

Mother grumbles at me. 'You work so hard, but what have you managed to achieve? Not even the girls' school. What's the point of carrying on? It would be better if you gave it up and came home.'

Her criticisms are never-ending. I can't sum them up in a single line. I store up what she says inside myself. I know I'll never forget it.

It's not only her fault. It's mine too. I've disappointed my mother.

My whole family resents me. I feel horribly alone. I think about school life. Keeping up with work is so hard when you can't see. So I think of giving up and coming home. But if this is how my family treats me . . . I no longer know what path to take. Who'll show me a good and generous road?

Tuesday 2 October.[59]
A fine day.

When we finish our homework this afternoon, my brother and I go off to our grandmother's where our father is working for our fifth uncle. As soon as we get there, we help our father shift a pile of earth. But when we want to go home again, he asks us to stay a little longer.

Our grandfather starts to tell stories about his youth, dating from the time when he fought against the Japanese.

There was one soldier who always wet his bed at night. The head of the squad beat him daily on account of this, but he couldn't seem to rid himself of his bad habit. The other soldiers wanted to stop the beatings, but they couldn't convince their chief. He just wouldn't listen. Worst of all, he tied the feet of the poor youth and hit him so much that he wept. At the end of it all, the soldier was sent home.

Our grandfather confesses that he loathed their head of squad. But he doesn't tell us anything of his own plight or bitterness. I think he was a real Red Army soldier. He won battles and he founded our family, which is a large one. I'm proud of him.

---

59 The children are off school for a week to mark the celebrations of the 1st of October national holiday.

Grandfather, I want to note it here, how very much I admire you, what a great and brave man I think you are. Throughout the world, from now on, it'll be recognised that you are one of the seeds of the Red Army.

Wednesday 3 October.
A fine day.

This afternoon, my brother Ma Yichao and I did the housework. Then we went to my fifth uncle's where my father has been working over the last few days in order to earn some money. We helped him as best we could.

When I looked at the clock, it was already five. I called my brother because we needed to go back to do our homework.

My fifth uncle's youngest son clung to our legs and whimpered. He wanted to come with us and see his mother. But I knew she wasn't there. She'd gone far away to harvest *fa cai*. His father wasn't there either and his two elder brothers had gone to stay with their maternal grandmother. I lifted him up in my arms and he started crying for real.

Seeing his tears, I was reminded of our childhood. When our parents weren't at home, we were pitiable creatures. I carried him to our house and asked myself why, when a child cries or is alone, he always shouts for 'Mother'. Why doesn't he ask for 'Father?'

Friday 5 October.
A grey day.

Market day today. Mother comes home from my maternal grandmother's. I go out to welcome her on the front porch. My mother's face is as black as coal and her lips are all cracked. She looks terrible. What's wrong with her? Usually when she come back from her mother's, she's happy, full of chat and laughter. But today . . .

Mother comes into the room and pours out all her resentments to us. 'When someone's poor, it's no good going back to your parents' family. Your grandfather loves me, yet since I left home, he's turned his back on me. He didn't ask me a single question, not even why I had come, or if it was cold on the way. He didn't say a single word.

'I'm really furious. I'm not going to go and see them any more. Listen to me, all three of you. Study well in order not to grow up like your father who has had to suffer the contempt of everyone around him all his life long. Forget the mocking laughter of your maternal grandfather. You'll have to be successful and show him how wrong he's been about everything.'

Saturday 6 October.
A grey day.

This afternoon I got bored. I called a few children over to play with me. We drew a round circle on the ground in the yard and ran about inside it. Suddenly my paternal grandfather arrived. He had come to eat watermelon. He had a little smile on his face and I accompanied him into the room and asked him to sit on the *kang*. I placed the low table on the *kang* and cut him a piece of watermelon and another of sweet melon. I handed the slices to him.

Crouched beside him, I watched him. He talked to me while he ate. He's already eighty and he doesn't have much time left. Wouldn't it be wonderful if he could live to be a hundred? By then, even if I haven't got a brilliant career, I'll certainly have some kind of job. And I'll be able to offer him a few last good days.

Monday 8 October.
A fine day.

The sixth lesson of the day is devoted to a daily class meeting. Here's what our main teacher, the one who teaches Chinese, taught us.

The first thing to respect, he told us, is school discipline. The second is our daily ten minutes of morning exercise. Thirdly, our studies: 'Those who have greater difficulty than others must start their work earlier and keep to a rigorous schedule, so that they know exactly when it's time to revise maths, and so on. Never think you're behind the others, just get on with it. You can always make progress by studying well.'

Why does each teacher talk about making progress? Now every time I think of the word, my hair stands on end. Do you know why? Because in the last English exam, I came second. It's cruel when I think of it.

But I've taken in what the teacher said today. I have to make a greater effort.

Wednesday 10 October.
A fine day.

This morning in our politics class, our teacher is very serious and the students listen attentively. I'm fascinated. He tells us a little story from his childhood. During a Chinese class, he had written, 'Teacher, you aren't a candle.[60] You are the sun.'

His teacher picked up his notebook and read the first line. Immediately he turned on him. 'I usually treat you well. How could you . . .'

'Please, teacher. Read the next sentence. You are the sun. If you were a candle, you'd eventually go out. You wouldn't be teaching us tomorrow. But if you're the sun, you can go on teaching and teaching every day.'

---

60 The Chinese regularly compare teachers to candles who consume themselves in giving light to others.

Thursday 11 October.
A fine day.

This morning, after our last class, I stay behind to do an essay. Suddenly the head of games comes in and tells me to go outside and join the ranks. 'All the others are already lined up. There's only you left.'

I go out to the sports ground and concentrate on standing very straight.

The other comrades have just started their games. Some are skipping with a rope, others are playing football, and still others are engaged in a game of tag between an eagle and chickens. I'd like to play too, but my heart isn't in it.

When I hear these children who aren't boarders talking about their families, I automatically think of my own. It makes me want to go straight home to see my mother and to ask her to make me a lovely dish of chips. That would be grand. I can already see myself chatting away happily to Mother.

Suddenly Ma Yichao runs past me, as fast as the wind. As soon as I see him, I stop having these dark thoughts and go off to play with the others.

I don't know what's wrong with me these days. I'm all upset about things. I don't know quite what I'm doing or thinking. My moods go up and down.

Wednesday 17 October.
A fine day.

We have a free period this afternoon. Our English teacher dictates a text to us. Two of the comrades can't manage it. The teacher hits them very hard with the leg of a chair. Bruises immediately appear on the arms and legs of the pupils.

This teacher wants us to do well, but he hits too hard. I think he enjoys it. I weep without showing the tears. I think their parents would be weeping, too, if they saw how badly their children were treated.

The teacher is in a rage and shouts, 'If you still haven't learned your lessons by the next period, I won't give you another chance. I'll only choose the brightest students to answer questions. And that'll be that. I won't come back to you at all.'

During the class, the teacher picks on me several times. My comrades look at me with envious eyes. They would do anything to get the better of me.

I mustn't worry about this. I mustn't let anything prevent me from attaining my goals and making good my plans for the future. I'll try and do something to change their jealous glances into admiring ones. I'll be as strong as my mother. When she encounters difficulties, she confronts them alone and no one dares laugh at her.

Failure is the mother of success. But it worries me to see the teacher striking the pupils. What will happen if they get hurt?

During the evening study period, these comrades managed to learn the words they hadn't known before. Why do they work better after they've been beaten? Their parents hope they'll become accomplished people, but after so many difficult years of study, how will they fulfil these expectations?

A skinny dog no longer manages to jump over a wall, even with help.

That's one of my mother's proverbs. I've never forgotten it. But it's only now that I grasp its full meaning.

Thursday 18 October.
A fine day.

Today, in Chinese class, the teacher asks us to write an essay on the theme of being in senior school. He takes the opportunity to explain to us the difference between the fast and the slower streams. The worst students in the fast class will be put into the slower class and the teacher will be penalised. That's why he wants us to work hard. All of us will reap the benefits. Finally he stops talking and tells us to start writing.

I finish my essay in a few minutes. All the comrades are surprised. 'We take two or three days to think over an essay, and you . . . you just dash one off.'

The teacher points out that even this isn't quick enough. 'You have to be like Ye Shengtao,[61] and practise speed and skill.'

The comrades make fun of me. 'Ye Shengtao is the cleverest man under the sun. Ma Yan comes second.'

Everyone laughs.

To tell the truth, there's nothing I'd like better than to be the second cleverest person in the world. If I had the chance I'd like to compete with grandfather Ye Shengtao. Who knows if my wish might be realised?

Friday 19 October.
Fine, but then grey.

Today my father has come to town for the market. He waits for me by the door while I'm still busy in class. I'm so happy because that means he probably has some money for me. Otherwise he wouldn't wait.

As soon as classes are over, I rush out to meet him. He gives me five yuan which I'll have to give to the teacher for books. He asks me if I've run out of bread.

I explain to him that the steamed bread is long finished. He buys two rolls, one for my brother and one for me. I hold on to mine. It's precious. I'll eat it tomorrow on the long road home.

61 A famous twentieth-century writer and educator, now dead.

When I get to the vegetable part of the market, I meet comrade Ma Yongmei. I borrowed a roll from her not long ago. She asks me to return what I owe her. I give her the bread rolls I'm holding. But she doesn't want that. She wants money. Where am I going to find money?

Friday 26 October.
A fine day.

My father gave us four yuan and told my brother and me to get a ride home on a tractor today. My parents are meant to have gone off to work again[62] and they were worrying about our safety.

But how in all conscience can I squander money on a tractor ride? My parents are working so hard, breaking their backs, bent over all the time, their faces fixed on the yellow earth. How can we possibly allow ourselves the extravagance of a tractor ride that is paid for with our parents' sweat? My brother and I prefer to walk home.

We set out at eleven in the morning and it is almost five when we finally reach home. We push open the door. Everything is quiet. The yard is empty. There's no one. No one here to say, 'Oh, at last. Here are my exhausted children. Quick. You must rest. Mother is going to prepare a meal for you . . .'

How I would love to hear Mother's voice. But Mother isn't here.

When it was dark, my brother went off to ask our paternal grandmother if she would keep us company. She didn't come and there's only us, my two brothers and me. We go to sleep silently on the *kang*. Outside, everything is quiet and we're very frightened. If Mother were here, I don't know what she would be talking about. It would probably be one of her funny stories. But she isn't here.

---

62 Both Ma Yan's parents have gone off to pick *fa cai* for two weeks at least. They sleep out under the stars, despite the October cold.

Even cuddled up in bed, we feel the cold. I don't know how Mother manages to sleep on the damp earth – especially since she's ill. What a terrible life she has. How much longer will she have to live this way? I so very much hope she'll soon be happy.

Saturday 27 October.
It's windy.

This morning I help my brother Ma Yichao to do his English home-work. He doesn't even know how to write the simplest words. I get angry and I can't prevent myself from giving him a slap. He starts to cry and doesn't want to go on. Suddenly, I start to cry, too . . .

Mother is always lecturing me: 'You have to take care of your little brother. You're bigger than he is and have a duty to help him. I send you to school and pay no attention to the costs. If you don't work well, not only do you not deserve the trouble I take for you, but you don't even deserve a week's bread.'

Her words play over and over in my mind. But my little brother doesn't work hard. I don't want to have to hear that he's been put back into the slow class.

While the two of us are crying, my second uncle comes to the house. He says that an official is busy inspecting one of our pieces of land. 'You should prepare this land for planting trees on,' he says to us. 'Aren't your parents here? Go and see your paternal grandmother then, and ask your fifth uncle to come and dig some holes for the trees.' Then he goes away.

What are we to do? Should I be going back to school or staying at home to attend to all this. I'm so confused, I can't even describe it.

And my mother isn't here . . . Every time I think of her, I want to cry.

Monday 29 October.
A fine day.

Good news today. On Wednesday we're going to have our mid-term exam. I'm very happy about it. I fully intend to demonstrate my abilities. I'm no worse than anyone else, apart from the fact that I eat and dress less well than they do. Some girls change their school clothes often. But I've only got one outfit, a pair of trousers and a white shirt, which I have to wash on Saturdays so that it's clean by Monday.

But what matter! I only want to study and pay tribute to my parents' hands.[63] Despite the cold, they're working far away from home for us. Why? For our future. And I mustn't disappoint them.

Tuesday 30 October.
A sombre day.

It's freezing today. My brother and I have no more bread. At lunchtime, the comrades are all eating and we have to stand by and grit our teeth.

Seeing my tears, my brother says, as if his heart were light, 'Wait, sister, I'm going to borrow some lunch tickets.' But I know he feels no better than I do. He simply wants to console me and stop me worrying about him. I go back to my dorm and sit on my bed and wait for him to return.

I'm dreaming of this bowl of yellow rice.

He takes a very long time to come back. Then he says, 'Sister, there's no more rice.'

He turns to leave. I watch my brother's receding back and I can't help letting the tears flow.

Do you know what hunger is? It's an unbearable pain.

I wonder when I'll stop experiencing hunger at school . . .

---

63 A common Chinese expression for gratitude.

Friday 2 November.
Wind.

All these last days we've been doing our mid-term exams. I think of nothing else, not even my sick mother who's working far away. Whatever she does, it's for our future. There's no question of disappointing the hope our parents have placed in us.

For the exams, some of the comrades have torn out pages of their books and hidden them in their pockets. They'll be punished. Others, as a precaution, write answers to difficult questions down the length of their arms. Do you think that's fair?

I haven't even opened my book. I remember that in primary school a teacher explained to us that before an exam, there's no point re-reading all your notes. It's better to relax, have fun. 'That's the best way to get good results,' he said.

I haven't altogether followed his advice. Instead, I sat on the edge of my bed and thought of my parents' suffering.

I can't disappoint them. I *will* do well.

Saturday 3 November.
A grey day.

The weekend starts today and I'm full of joy. I hope that my parents have come home. I'll tell them all about the mid-term exams.

I'm busy planning all kinds of projects when a comrade whispers: 'The politics teacher knows our exam results.'

But another comrade is furious. 'He doesn't. He only knows how the best students did, not the results of the dunces like us who aren't ranked among the top students.'

I hurry over to the teacher's house. It's already full of students. I've only just come in when I hear the teacher's voice. 'Ma Yan got 114 points in maths. She's come top of all six classes. She got 90 points in Chinese . . . The English results haven't come in yet.'

I'm so overjoyed, I burst into tears. I don't know where so many tears can come from. My vision is blurred, but I go outside again.

I'm so moved, I still can't even find words to describe how I feel. Never have I had a moment like this one. Never will I forget it.

Monday 5 November.
A fine day.

At the class meeting, the teacher pinned up our exam results. He explained working methods to us.

'When you're asked to put the answer to a question between parentheses, you don't need to show us the working out of the whole problem.'

I know that that's directed at me. He goes on.

Ma Yan in the second row of her classroom.
She managed to become one of the top pupils in her year.

'For multiple-choice questions, just choose one answer. There's no point ticking two or more. Some students often do this. I hope you won't make these same mistakes next time round. For the calculations, use the most economical method. To make an analysis, you must read the question carefully and think . . .'

When he's finished with these explanations, he asks the students to give him the results of each exam, as well the total, since he needs to fill out a form.

At the end of the day, I have a total of 299 points. I come second. Someone who is repeating the year comes first.[64] Tears of joy pour from my eyes. The teacher congratulates me and says everyone should take me as a model.

But the more he talks, the sadder I become, because Mother has had to go far off to work. Everything the teacher said today will stay etched on my mind. If I follow his advice, I think I'll be able to overcome my difficulties.

Next time, I shall try to come first.

During class today, the politics teacher compliments me once more. He admits that up until now he had paid no attention to me, noticing neither my qualities nor my faults.

'In her mid-term exams, comrade Ma Yan has shown lots of potential – potential I hadn't suspected she had. I judged her wrongly. I have already told her what I think of her work. If you don't believe me, ask her. You should know that a comrade of ours wrote in a composition: "When we hadn't done well in an exam the teacher insulted us, complaining that he had taught a class of idiots and all in vain." This same girl went on to say, "Teacher, you

64 This detail is important to Ma Yan whose best subjects are maths, Chinese and English.

shouldn't underestimate us: failure is the mother of success." This is both a piece of advice she offers to your teacher and the expression of her own feelings. This girl is in our class.'

Everyone is staring at me. It's true, I wrote those words. If I did well in these exams, it's largely because of what this teacher said. If he hadn't called us idiots, I would certainly not have gone on to get the results I did.

Wednesday 7 November.
A fine day.

I'm so hungry, I could eat anything. Anything at all.

When I talk about hunger, I instantly think of my mother. I don't know if she's got home safely. Me, I'm happy enough coming to school every day and being hungry. But Mother has to run up mountain slopes every day. And I don't know how she's faring. On top of it all, she's ill.

It's three weeks since I've seen her. I think of her all the time.

I'm terribly hungry. There's been no bread or vegetables since Tuesday. When I eat my rice now, there's nothing to go with it.

I even took some food from a comrade's bowl without asking her. When she came back to the dormitory, she called me all manner of names.

What can I say to her? When I hear her sounding off, I think of my father who left my brother and me four yuan. We've been living on that for three weeks, and I still have one left over in my pocket. My stomach is all twisted up with hunger, but I don't want to spend that yuan on anything so frivolous as food. Because it's money my parents earn with their sweat and blood.

I have to study well so that I won't ever again be tortured by hunger and lack of money. When I have a job, I'll certainly be able to guarantee some happy times for my parents. I'll never let them go far away to work for us again.

Thursday 8 November.
A fine day.

It's market day. In the English class, I'm sitting next to the window. Suddenly, I see a shadow from the corner of my eyes. I lift my head. Behind the window, I see Mother. I'm staggered. It's so long since I've seen her. Even through the window I can see that her face is all black and swollen.

The class comes to an end without my noticing. In any case, I've taken nothing in. It's not important. I'll ask the teacher what I've missed at the next lesson. First, I have to find Mother.

Father and Mother are waiting for me in the street. I'm so happy! It's so long since we've all been together. Father, Mother, my brother and me. We walk down the street, all together. We talk about all kinds of things and forget about our stomachs. Suddenly Mother taps her forehead: 'But you two, you haven't eaten yet?'

We shake our heads.

She takes us to the market. She buys us vegetable soup for fifty fen and we also get bread to dunk in the bowl.

After we've eaten, we go off to buy winter clothes. With good padded clothes, we won't be cold. We each get a jacket and shoes and socks. In no time at all we've spent over a hundred yuan. What a pity! I feel both happy and sad. Money is so hard to earn and so easy to spend. You don't even notice it going.

I don't know how Mother and Father have earned these hundred yuan, how many days it took, how many tens of hours, hundreds of minutes, thousands and thousands of seconds. And I spent all this hard-earned wealth as if it were nothing at all.

When I grow up, what won't I do for my parents!

Friday 9 November.
A nice day.

Tomorrow, we go home and I'm so happy.

Tonight, during the study hour, there was a blackout. All the comrades were thrilled. They were happy not to have electricity to see by: a whole hour in which to have fun.

But I'm happy just to go home, to sit down with my mother and talk things over.

Several weeks have passed since we were all together at home. This time when we get there, I'm going to ask my parents how they spent every single day, and especially how Mother's health is. I think her pains started again when she was up in the mountains.

When I saw her in the market, with her hands all swollen and her face black, I understood that her attacks had begun again. And despite all that, she slept on the damp ground. Why does she do it? It certainly isn't for herself.

No, it's for us, for our future, the work we'll be able to get. I have to work hard in order to merit the hope my parents place in me, and so that I can make the second half of their lives better than the first.

Sunday 11 November.
A fine day.

This morning at about five o'clock, Mother got up to prepare our food, worried that we would be hungry. Then she woke us. We got dressed, had a wash and sat down to breakfast.

While I ate, I noticed that my mother's eyes, face, feet and hands were all swollen. I asked her what was wrong and she said, 'Nothing, nothing. Maybe I got up too quickly . . .'

I know that's not the reason. Her attacks are bad again.

I ask her if the swelling is caused by her illness.

159

'What illness?' She stares at me. 'I must have woken you up too early. You're still all mixed up. Eat. Quickly . . .'

A vehicle pulls up and my mother makes it an excuse to put an end to my questions. I know she's running away from them, just so that I don't worry about her. And so that I will study well and become a useful member of society.

I will work well. Otherwise I won't deserve Mother's hard-working hands which have prepared our breakfast this morning.

Monday 12 November.
A fine day.

What I really want is to go home, straight away, without waiting for the weekend. I want to see Mother's face and her hands again. Because I know that she's going away to work again. Far away . . . I don't want her to go away, but I don't know how to prevent it.

Last week, when we got home, Mother wanted to see my report card. I showed her the exam papers. After she had looked at them, she smiled.

'I haven't spent all this money for nothing,' she concluded. 'You haven't disappointed my expectations in the least.'

She looked at my brother's exam papers too and she exploded, 'How can you possibly think you deserve the bread you take away with you every week? How do you think I managed to get through the exhaustion of the mountains? My hope in you, that's how. And now look at the results! How can I help but be disappointed. And sad.'

When I think of my mother, I really want to go home. I feel like asking for permission to leave. But even if I go home, I fear I may already have missed her. She's probably left already to harvest *fa cai*. I can only wish her good health. Because if her illness starts again, there's no one there to look after her. This time Father isn't going with her. He's staying at home to look after the house and the fields.

How I hope that her attacks don't start again. She only had a two- or three-day break at home before setting off again to try and earn some more money. How I love it when we're all together as a family eating and talking. I really want to have a warm and happy family! But the heavens don't seem to want it and they force me to live in melancholy and pain.

But the unhappiest person of all is Mother. All year long, she has to leave home to work far away. That's where her illness came from. From going off to earn the keep of the three of us children. And my brother hasn't brought honours home from school. So of course she's sad.

I have to carry on working hard, so as not to disappoint her. The biggest wishes in my life are that she gets better and that our family is at last together for good.

If ever I succeed in life, my success will equally be Mother's. I'll always remember her.

Why am I always so unhappy, why do my tears never dry? Tell me why? Will I only succeed when I have no tears left? And if they don't dry up, is that a sign that I won't ever succeed?

I must persist on this difficult path.

Tuesday 13 November.
A fine day.

I don't know where Mother spent last night, whether she slept on the damp ground or on a rocky promontory at the edge of a road. I'm only certain of one thing. I know she didn't sleep well. The temperature has gone right down to below zero. On top of that, there are her stomach problems.

I know how hard it is to pick *fa cai*. I did it once with my father. It was still summer. At one in the morning, the tractor we were on ran out of fuel. We had to get off and sleep in a field on the bare ground. In no time at all, I was covered in dust. It crawled up my nostrils. I breathed it. I couldn't get to sleep. I sat up and counted the stars in the sky.

I thought of a story we'd once had to read called 'The Child who Counts the Stars'. Once upon a time there was a boy who leaned against his grandmother at night and counted the stars. His grandmother told him the stars were innumerable, uncountable. But the boy answered that provided he believed he could, he would somehow manage to count them.

I didn't really understand his point when I first read the story.

That night in the open air, when I saw so many stars, I really wanted more than anything else to lean against Mother and count them. But I understood that it was impossible to count the stars. It was the first time I think I realised how vast the natural world is.

It was also the first time in my life that I had travelled so far. I already missed home. I felt so pitifully small . . . and so very sad.

For her family, for our future, Mother has gone off to earn money against all the odds. She makes such an effort. And she lives so miserably. She's so tired.

I must above all work hard in order to succeed, so that Mother can at last have an easier life, can at last get rid of her pain and exhaustion. I hope that my wish comes true quickly and that Mother soon has a happier life.

Thursday 15 November.
A fine day.

This morning, during gym, a new kind of exercise: we go off to run in the streets instead of staying in the school yard.

Our class trails class four. We run as fast as we can to catch up with them and get ahead. By the time we do, I'm covered in sweat. The locals come out of their houses to watch us.

It's really great being a student. The only problem is that our parents suffer, especially my mother. If we don't work well, when our classroom is full of sunshine and our school full of joy, how will we ever merit all the efforts our parents make on our behalf?

For the children of rich families, one day more or less makes no difference at all. For me, the child of a poor family, every day brings new trials with it. Not in terms of studying, because there I'm at the top of the class, but because of the kind of life we lead.

So I have to study hard in order not to suffer from hunger in the future.

Of course, the most important thing of all is my mother. I don't want her going off to work far from home any more. Our family will be happy, united. We'll have no more problems.

I'm going to work assiduously, pursue my goal without slacking and my dream of building a bright future for my homeland.

Friday 16 November.
A fine day.

I haven't seen our politics teacher for several days. I'd very much like to see him, look at his face and hear his voice. His presence and his words always make me very happy. Somehow he offers consolation, assuages my sufferings and my problems. That's why I so want to see him come into the room. He has the ability to comfort anyone who is worried or unhappy.

I'm always full of suffering and worries. No sooner do I lower my head than Mother's words come into my mind, together with her ravaged hands. Why does this word 'mother' leap into my mind so very often?

I like the politics teacher's way of using words as well as his manner. But I don't like the subject he teaches us. All we ever do is discuss heroes of history, patriotism, Taiwan and morality. In each of his classes, I secretly do my homework for other subjects. The teacher often says we should listen carefully. But I can't seem to correct my bad habits.

Today, when we had a lesson with him, he picked me out, asked me to stand up. He wondered if I could answer a question. I shook my head. He let me sit down again. I know what he wanted to ask me: Could I listen more carefully during his class? That's why I refused to answer.

He shows me a lot of consideration and I always disappoint him. From now on, I'm going to change my habits. I don't want to let him down any more, or make him unhappy.

Monday 19 November.
A fine day.

At noon, after classes, the comrades go home to eat. Since I'm a Hui, this is a fasting period for me. I've started Ramadan. This gives me a little free time.

In the street where I walk, I feel terribly alone. I think of Mother again. If only she were here . . . How wonderful that would be! Because everything I do is in relation to her.

If I make some kind of mistake, and haven't checked with her for her advice first, she chides me all day. Sometimes I resent her. But when I think about it, I know that she's doing it all for my own good. I mustn't get angry with her. If I hadn't followed her advice, where would I be today? I would lack maturity and I would understand nothing of the good things in life. If I hadn't had Mother teaching me, with all her criticisms, I wouldn't know what a fen or a yuan was, nor where they came from.

Without Mother, there would be no Ma Yan. I must be grateful to the woman who allowed her daughter to grow, to mature, to become herself.

Thursday 22 November.
A fine day.

This week has flown by. It's already Thursday and I don't know how we got here. I have this great wish to go home.

There's news in the village. We're putting in place the measures which will allow the fields to be planted with trees. Each week, when I go home, the village has changed a little. The hills have acquired holes at regular intervals. In the spring, we'll plant the trees. All of us will be really excited then. Our land will turn green again.

I think that in a few years, or maybe a few decades, the landscape will have changed completely. These days, everywhere you look, there's only yellow earth. If you walk up to the high plateau to look down at the village, all you can see is yellow barrenness, a dried-out terrain. It's not even a landscape. To tell the truth, there's nothing to see.

Nor does the economy produce anything. Only *fa cai* allows one to live at all. The situation has to change. In the future, our village will be green. Its inhabitants will have acquired knowledge and will know how to build solid houses. If I work hard at school, when I grow up, I'll be able to devote my energy and skills to improving the cruel life of the villagers.

Wednesday 28 November.
A bright day.

This evening, after classes, a friend invited me home. She's like the little sister I would have liked to adopt. Her family lives fairly close to the school. There's only one valley to cross. On the way we meet several comrades who look happy. Seeing their joy, I too would like to be home. They all say how agreeable it is to sleep in one's own home.

At first when I get to my friend's house, I feel ill at ease. But her parents are very nice and ask me lots of questions. When we got there, her father came out on the porch to welcome us. At my place, when we have guests, it's my mother who welcomes them. Father stands by near her, because he's not very savvy about dealing with people.

No sooner had we come in, than my friend's parents brought us two bowls of meat. The steam was still rising from them. Then came fruit.

I envy my friend having a family that's so hospitable and happy. She doesn't have to worry about them. And they eat meat! I don't know how long it's been since we ate rice with meat at home. At the next market, I'd love to buy a little meat for Mother.

Tuesday 4 December.
Light snow.

Snow is floating in the air. I miss my village. We're in the midst of a history lesson and the teacher goes on and on. I'm sitting near the window. When I turn my head, I can see snowflakes fluttering through the air before drifting to the ground. It takes me back to my childhood.

It was a very cold winter morning. Snow was falling thickly. My parents weren't home. They had gone far away to harvest *fa cai*.

My mother's illness started that winter. It was a hard and bitterly cold one. The snow rose high all around us, more snow than I had ever seen since I could remember. When the snow and wind stopped, my brothers, my grandmother who was about seventy then, and I, filled our underground cistern with snow, so that there would be no shortage of water during the winter.

Every Saturday when I'm at home, Mother asks me to collect up the donkey droppings. And I never manage it. She reminds me then of that snowbound winter. She says, 'You were so little, but so brave. Now you've become weak and useless. What shall I do with you?'

Every time Mother talks like this, I remember the cold of that winter. I don't know how Mother and Father survived it. I don't know how I managed to carry all those bundles of snow. I don't really recall much except the cold and the snow. I only hope that I'm braver now than I was then.

Friday 7 December.
A grey day.

The fair is on today. My heart light, classes seemed to race past much more quickly than usual. I floated to the market, carried by one great hope. Last Saturday, Mother promised she'd be there today. Since Ramadan is almost over, she has to come to market to buy presents for people and invite an aged person home to break the fast.

The wind whistles and it's so cold that you can't take your hands out of your pockets. As I walk through the streets I see people of all kinds shivering with cold. I look for Mother but I can't find her. The tears start to run down my face. They freeze into ice. I meet a lot of women wearing a white kerchief just like Mother's. I'm tempted to stop one of them, take her hand, call her 'Mother' . . . but as soon as I step forward, I see that it isn't my mother and I stop myself.

I have the feeling someone is calling me. I turn round and see Father. My heart is suddenly less empty. But he isn't Mother. My father comes up to me, mutters a few words and heads off. When it's Mother, she launches a barrage of questions at me. I love that. It's so engaging. And then, it's so difficult to leave her.

Why do I spend so much time thinking about Mother?

Thursday 13 December.
A fine day.

It's market day again today. I'm very happy. I'm sure Mother will go and break the Ramadan fast with her maternal grandmother. But at the market, when I look for her, I can't find her. She hasn't come. The tears pour down my face. What a disappointment. Every market day, I come in the hope of seeing her and she isn't here . . .

I'm walking with my head down when I see my maternal grand-father and my father. They're talking enthusiastically. But they're dressed in rags. Their clothes are dirty, their shoes full of holes. They look so ugly to me! On top of it all, they've got napkins round their waists, which makes them look even more grotesque.

I don't know what my grandfather has eaten on this holy day, but as his granddaughter, I should be performing a pious act on his behalf. So I buy him fifty fen worth of apples, so that he can cele-brate the end of the fast with them. But he disappears before I can give him his present.

At the vegetable market I meet my maternal grandmother. My grandfather asked her to buy some apples, she tells me. So I give her the apples I bought, and on top of it, go and buy pears for her. I've spent a great deal of money in very little time. It's not that I wanted to, but I couldn't do otherwise.

I turn back towards school. In front of the market entrance I see an old woman who reminds me of my paternal grandmother. I buy fifty fen of pears. She, too, looks over seventy: she's arrived at the age where one must have feelings of respect towards her.

I've used up all the money I intended to spend on a notebook. Apart from the thirty-five yuan I spent in the district capital when I went to sit the entrance exams, this is the first time since primary school that I've spent so much money all at once. Two yuan! But I had to. To honour a great feast-day you have to buy good things to eat, beautiful clothes for the whole family. I have little enough apart from my sense of responsibility and the piety that lives in my heart.

WHAT HAPPENED NEXT

The Solidarity of Readers

When the French daily newspaper *Libération* carried an extract from Ma Yan's diary in January 2002, readers responded in great numbers. They were touched by the fate of this Chinese girl, moved by her rebellion and her desperate desire to continue her schooling. Readers proposed financial help: some offered to finance her education, however long it took.

A number of people attributed their reaction to the fact that they too had had a difficult past. Others acknowledged that they suffered from a kind of rich-guilt while still others acted out of a spirit of pure generosity.

One reader proposed: 'Couldn't we do what certain NGOs do – organise a system by which a sum is sent to her family every month so that Ma Yan can go to school? This is in no way an act of giving alms. Let's for once listen to Mao who says "If we give a net to a fisherman, he can catch fish!" This money would act as Ma Yan's net.'

So, in the summer of 2002, we created a fund called Children of Ningxia, which would help the children of families in need to go back to school. There was no question of a vast administrative apparatus or a new non-governmental organisation, just a simple system for sponsoring children.[65] The only condition of the sponsorship was that the children wrote to us once a term to give us news of their studies and tell us how things were progressing.

---

65 An association called Children of Ningxia was created during the summer of 2002 to organise the sponsorship: 45 rue Notre-Dame-de-Nazareth, 75003 Paris, France

Ma Yan's Letter

Dear Uncles and Aunts,[66]

How are you?[67] I received your letter on 17 February 2002. That day my father had gone to town for the market and he found the letter at the post office. He opened it right away, but there were a few characters he couldn't recognise. Back at home, he asked me to read it. When I had finished the reading, I don't know why, but I broke out in a sweat, as if all my strength had gone . . . Maybe it was because I was just too moved, too, too happy.

Father said, when he had finished reading the letter, that he no longer knew if he was walking on earth or in the sky, because he felt as if his body was floating. Mother added, 'Finally, the heavens have opened their eyes. I didn't cry for no reason while I was up in the mountains. My tears, then, were the result of pain and sadness. Now, they come from joy. I wish you a very good year and convey all my gratitude.'

After reading your letter, I really understood what joy in this world means: friendship and the meaning of life. I thank all the people who have set out to help me. I am thrilled that young French people want to be my friends. I would like to write to them, phone them immediately, but I have neither their addresses nor phone numbers. Then, too, they don't speak Chinese. I hope that you'll

---

66 The way Ma Yan addresses the sponsors of her schooling is a respectful form of address from children to adults.
67 In English in the Chinese letter.

give them my address: I would like to be their friend, their best friend. I say 'Thank you'[68] to all of them.

You said that you could help other children from families in need. I'm so very, very pleased at that. For me, my problems are now behind me. Let them, too, complete their schooling and fulfil their dreams. All my thanks.

Soon I'm going back to school. I shall work very hard not to disappoint all your expectations.

I wish you great success in this year of the horse.

Ma Yan
19 February 2002

---

68 In English.

Study Grants

We're on our third trip. Our goal is a limited one. We want to offer several children of families in need a study grant apportioned from the funds we raised around Ma Yan's case. Our first stop is the senior school of the rural commune of Yuwang, run by a man whose good-will far exceeds his means.

He tells us a startling statistic: the number of students between the first and second school terms fell from 994 to 912. The drop in numbers is due to the financial straits in which peasant families find themselves. Of the pupils who passed the senior school entrance examination, almost one-tenth can't afford to attend. Nothing could be done about it.

The school's head introduces us to six girls who were among those who won't be returning for the second term. Girls are the first victims in poor families.[69] One of the school's best students is a girl disabled by polio. Her parents can't afford to send her here any more.

Now these six girls and Ma Yan can be assured of enough funds to continue their schooling thanks to the French readers. They

---

69 In the south of the country in the province of Guangxi, Françoise Grono-Wing, a Frenchwoman who works for an organization called Couleurs de Chine, runs a programme for pupils from the ethnic minorities of the region. She launched the charity in 1998 because when she went round the region's schools, she found hardly a single girl. Now she has helped 1,200 Chinese girls to attend school through a sponsorship programme. See the website:

www.actualitesolidarite.com/reportage/ong/couleurchine/couleurchine.htm

Ma Yan and the six pupils who received grants funded by
the readers of the newspaper *Libération*.

pose together for a photo (above). After trying to be serious for
Wang Zheng's camera for a moment, they burst into joyous smiles.

The children have to pay registration fees of about 200 yuan a
term for a very austere and basic education. That sum is doubled for
the two-thirds of students who have to board since they come from
neighbouring villages. They must bring their rice and a little money
to buy vegetables. The school's head tells us that though the poorest can be exempted from registration fees, he can do nothing about
the cost of their food.

This amount represents a considerable expense for many families
whose annual income doesn't rise above four to five hundred yuan
and who sometimes have several children to educate.

The next stage of our trip takes us to the village of Zhangjiashu.

The secretary of the Yuwang Communist Party,
Mr Luo, and villagers crossing a field.

Very quickly all its inhabitants gathered in front of Ma Yan's house. They were awaiting our arrival impatiently. We already have the names of several children whom we'd like to help – beginning with the girl we met on our first journey who raced off, screaming her wish to go back to school. It's difficult to forget the expression of that level of pain.

Other names come to light as soon as we start talking things over with the villagers. But we have to take heed of the local authorities, who have supported our project. The old village head, the secretary of the Communist Party and the imam are among them.

We have six grants left to hand out and we ask for suggestions. They start to negotiate, crouching in the field in front of Ma Yan's house. The two men are rivals, both interested in serving their own groups but finally they present us with a list, evidently the result of compromise.

Ma Yan, looking at the article about herself in *Libération*.

We meet each child and each family and it's certainly clear to us that these people are in need.

But it is also clear that we won't be able to satisfy all expectations. Unsurprisingly our presence created as many frustrations as satisfactions.

One night, in the pitch darkness when we were driving home from visiting one of the families whom we hoped to help, we had to brake hard to stop ourselves from running down a kneeling woman, arms stretched out in the shape of a cross. She heard the car's engine and she knows who we are. She finds it unjust that her children haven't been selected and she has no other way of attracting our attention. Feeling dreadful, we none the less have to say no to her. We just haven't the means to help everyone.

Pierre Haski with Ma Yan in front of her house.

At the turn of a road, we saw a slogan painted in a school yard. 'Even if there's not enough rice in your bowl, send your child to school.'

Elsewhere, we saw another slogan: 'If a child doesn't go to school, it's the parents' fault.'

This blaming of parents seems harsh in the light of the fact that the state has failed to fulfil its duties, not to mention the natural catastrophe of five consecutive years of drought.

The Hope of Education

She got up at three in the morning and walked for four hours across the hills. The cold was glacial. It hadn't lessened despite the fact that it was March. Once she reached Yuwang, she found out where 'the foreigners' were staying. At seven-thirty, she was waiting for us to emerge from our hotel rooms.

Still shivering, the courageous girl explained how she heard that we had returned to Zhangjiashu with subsidies for children to go to school. Upset about not being able to continue her education, she has come to plead her case before we leave the region. Since her parents are off harvesting *fa cai* in Inner Mongolia, she begged her uncle to come with her so that she wouldn't have to walk the distance alone at night.

Next to her stood a couple accompanied by a shy young girl. They too have come to plead. The father suffered an injury when he fell off a tractor heading towards the *fa cai*-picking region and this has destroyed the family's fragile finances. So they have come to us in the hope of obtaining a subsidy for their daughter, a school friend of Ma Yan's.

The scale of hope that our modest enterprise has raised, makes us confront the immensity of need in this region.

A huge proportion of the country has remained underdeveloped and the western provinces in particular have been left untouched by the economic boom elsewhere. But the increasingly opulent shop windows of Beijing and Shanghai have an anaesthetising effect. They disguise the harsh reality of life for many in the cities, let alone a thousand kilometres away.

The Fourth Trip

July 2002. We've come back to Zhangjiashu for the fourth time. When we reach the village, we see people working in a field. As soon as she spots us, a girl runs towards our car. She's one of the children who have received a grant. She's come back to help her parents in the fields during the school holidays. But her grades have been excellent and she'll go back to school next term.

Very quickly a group forms at Ma Yan's house. Among the many children, we recognise several who have happily managed to return to the work benches of their school. There are many parents, too, who have come to make the case for their own children. In such a poor community, aid brings as much disappointment as it solves problems. The situation is tricky to manage: no one understands that we're not the United Nations, but simply the modest representatives of a small group of Europeans moved by the story we read in a diary.

Ma Yan's mother greets us, but she's in the midst of one of the attacks of stomach cramps Ma Yan describes in her diary. We decide to take her, together with Ma Yan, to the hospital in Yinchuan, which is 400 kilometres further north. There a doctor diagnoses a stomach ulcer, complicated by other ills caused by the lack of medical care, but also due to insufficient hygiene in her village which has no running water.

This trip, motivated by a medical emergency, becomes something of an initiation rite for Ma Yan. She has never before left her rural district in the south of Ningxia. She now finds herself in a city

Ma Yan in Yinchuan

which, without having the splendour of Shanghai or the power of Beijing, has none the less modernised rapidly over these last years. With eyes wider than saucers, she watches girls in miniskirts astride scooters. Everywhere there are garish advertising posters, restaurants, clothes and electrical appliance shops stretching as far as she can see along grand avenues . . . For the first time she is face to face with a China she has only ever glimpsed on television. Never before has it been quite so clear to her how distant her day-to-day life is from all this.

In the hotel bathroom Ma Yan discovers hot running water and all the other modern commodities: shower, bath, toilet, sink. She uses soap for the first time. At home, all they have is detergent.

Another first is the lift, and then the escalator. On the fourth floor of the department store where the customers are caught in a consumer frenzy, Ma Yan is overtaken by vertigo. She recovers in the covered market, which is rather better supplied than the modest

Ma Yan and her mother waving goodbye
before returning to their village.

one in Yuwang . . . She tastes Coca-Cola, ice cream and in a restaurant – a Muslim one on her mother's insistence – she stuffs herself with lamb to the point of indigestion.

Ma Yan learns quickly. To her mother, whose eyes are even wider than the schoolgirl's, Ma Yan says, 'Don't bend over like that. You look like a peasant . . .'

When we have to leave, she confides in us that this trip has proved an 'unforgettable experience'. It has made her think hard about her life and her ambitions.

Since the publication of the article about Ma Yan, first twenty and then thirty children have benefited from European sponsorship. This is a drop of water in an ocean of need, but it makes all the difference to these children. All of them wrote to us to say that school was going well.

The spontaneous gesture of Ma Yan's mother when she put the notebooks in our hands, a little like the way one tosses a message in a bottle to the high seas in desperate times, has had consequences far greater than she could have imagined. Her life, the life of her family and those of many other children in this forgotten village at the end of the world, have been transformed.

How Things Have Changed

In Ma Yan's little house in the village of Zhangjiashu, a photograph of a class of French schoolchildren has pride of place on the wall next to the family photographs. On the back of the photo, the pupils have written: 'Carry on with your schooling. French children are with you . . .'

These children were among the first in France to have come to Ma Yan's aid. Emmanuelle, one of their teachers, had read them the article in *Libération* which appeared in January 2002. 'When I finished reading it, several of the pupils were in tears. One of them put up his hand and asked, "What can we do to help, Miss?"'

The students collected money throughout the school and they sent 100 euros to help Ma Yan and other Chinese children get back to school.

The picture of the French high-school class on Ma Yan's wall and the story of Ma Yan on the walls of the French school – this bridge between two universes which would never otherwise have touched each other – is part of the 'miracle' of this whole adventure. Ma Yan's diary struck a chord in these children and indeed in France as a whole. The result was an even greater solidarity with the children in the impoverished province of Ningxia.

As soon as the diary was published, the responses started pouring in. A teacher in the east of France, whose pupils came from a particularly poor background and had real schooling difficulties, wrote to us to say that he regularly used the story of Ma Yan with his pupils. 'Some of them were genuinely touched by Ma Yan's story and expressed a desire to send her something or at least to try and correspond with her.' What resulted were some twenty letters, drawings and poems addressed to Ma Yan. Each of them had a ballpoint pen taped to it – a response to the diary entry in which she says she hadn't eaten so that she could buy a pen.

Dozens of letters from young French people, moved and indeed disturbed by Ma Yan's story, came to us and through us went on to Ma Yan. For a lot of teenagers, this was their first encounter with the 'real world', and with an untenable injustice.

Fifteen-year-old Alice, a pupil in a very good Parisian school, sent us a long email in which she wrote:

I realised, reading this book, that we in the West know nothing about the misery of others . . . It's true, we know they're very poor, but we don't really understand the degree of poverty, the true hardships in which they live . . . I find it loathsome. I'm even sometimes ashamed of myself. For example, there I am like any other teenager, preoccupied with my little love problems, my poor grades, my fights with my parents, the new jeans I want to buy . . . or I find myself complaining because my parents forgot to buy my favourite dessert . . . It's ridiculous. To think that at the very same moment, Ma Yan is busy thinking about things that are so much more serious: 'I must do well in my studies! Mother only lives so that my brothers and I can have a life better than hers . . .' or 'when will I see Mother again, now that she's gone to harvest *fa cai*?'

The teenage magazine *L'Actu* voted Ma Yan 'best-loved of the year 2002'.

Indeed, the publication of Ma Yan's diary led to a great deal of support for the Association for the Children of Ningxia, set up in France in 2002. This charitable grouping emerged from the kernel of

185

readers who had responded to the first article in *Libération*. The initial handful of members had increased to three hundred by the end of that year. Donations allowed it to expand its work. Thus, at the beginning of the second school term in February 2003, the association gave out forty-two grants, mostly to pupils at the senior school in Yuwang and the primary school in Zhangjiashu. Children who would have had to leave school could now continue their education.

The subsidy also served to establish a library in the senior school for the first time. By September 2003, this poor rural college could boast an Information Technology programme with twenty-two computers, thanks to the help of French students in Beijing and Hong Kong. These priorities were at the behest of the school's head who told us that he wanted computers. 'Because if my pupils leave school without having touched a computer, we will have created the new illiterates of the twenty-first century.'

Other projects are under discussion, such as the digging of a well in Zhangjiashu since water is such a vital problem. The SARS epidemic in China in the spring of 2003 made us ask ourselves whether it was also imperative to run a programme of health education for the villagers, since their health is certainly at risk.

It is difficult to take on board the utter change in Ma Yan's life. A few months ago this girl never had enough to eat and was threatened with having to give up school and take up the miserable life of a village peasant. Now she's a celebrity in France and to a certain extent in China as well. Thanks to the royalties from her book, she can eat her fill. The advantages and disadvantages of all this have yet to be fully measured.

A Chinese magazine in December 2002 summed up the impact the book has had on its young heroine. 'Ma Yan, happy, but stressed out!' Happy, most definitely, because she and her family have moved out of dire need, have proper winter clothes, have bought some sheep, and also a new television which sits at the very centre of the single room which is still their home. Happy, too, because she knows that the education she values so much is now secure for her. University, too, if she works well – something which was almost unthinkable for a native of this impoverished village.

But she's also anxious, as the magazine said. First of all, because in this village, like anywhere else in the world, success provokes jealousy and hostility. And also because Ma Yan has become a 'model', an example to her comrades, which means she isn't allowed to make mistakes. On top of it all she's had to assume a status that is challenging for a fifteen-year-old peasant girl: it has involved being flown to Beijing to talk on national television. And in March 2004, she was flown to Paris for a Book Fair, and there she was interviewed by media from around the world. The *New York Times* said of her diary, 'Thanks to its publication, her family is no longer poor, and 250 Ningxia youngsters, mostly girls, now have scholarships to continue studying.'

To my great surprise, the story of Ma Yan had real resonance in China too – whereas we had thought that the misfortunes of a Chinese girl would seem banal to other Chinese. Several Chinese newspapers wrote articles and even features based on the village – though it's difficult to know whether what had brought them there is the fate of China's disinherited peasantry or curiosity about Ma Yan's success in France. It hardly matters. Pertinent articles appeared in serious papers like *Nanfang Zhomou*, the Canton weekly, and the Shanghai daily, *Wen Hui Bao*. Both posed the problems of the forgotten peasantry and the fact that access to education had become a luxury impossible to attain.

CCTV, national television, interviewed Ma Yan and her mother no less than three times for different programmes, which gave her story extraordinary impact. Her diary described as 'legendary' by the Chinese media is now published in China by Huaxia Publishing House. The first print run was 100,000 copies. Even Ma Yan's mother has begun to learn how to write.

But this courageous and intelligent young woman has taken on these changes with modesty and generosity. When we visited her in February 2003, she gave us a handwritten letter in which she made a solemn announcement.

I'm an ordinary pupil. I had help from certain friends. Today I want to offer love so that more poor students can enter into the world of knowledge which is school. So that they can slowly make their dreams come true. So that they can build a better future for our country, our native land. If everyone offers up a little love, the world will be better. I want to give 25% of all my royalties from Ma Yan's Diary to the Association for the Children of Ningxia.

Pierre Haski
Beijing, 18 May 2003

APPENDICES

Our Photographer, Wang Zheng

The photographer Wang Zheng was our point of entry to Ningxia. A French friend in Beijing, Sarah Neiger, had discovered his unpublished photographs while she was researching an exhibition destined for Nice. Wang Zheng's black-and-white images moved us: he had not only captured the dry, rural landscape of the interior of China, but also a vibrant Islamic world. The China of his photographs was unusual, unknown.

When we met in Beijing, Wang Zheng explained his work to us. He is a warm man of around forty and himself comes from the southern tip of Ningxia. His father had joined Mao Zedong in the 'liberated zone' of Yanan, part of the neighbouring province of Shaanxi at the end of the 1930s, when the Long March of the retreating Communist army took it across the mountains in the south of Ningxia.

After the creation of the People's Republic in 1949, his father, who is now over eighty, became a Communist official in his home district. Wang Zheng, however, moved closer to Islam, dominant in Ningxia.

Wang Zheng knows that the region is condemned by its hostile climate and geography. He has chosen to preserve it photographically. Over the last five years he's travelled back and forth over the south of Ningxia, a region unknown to the Chinese themselves. To his photographs, he has added another important documentary medium: he makes lists of clans and families, and notes their personal and collective histories, thereby creating a bank of information about these arid villages just at the moment when their population is shrinking.

Ploughing through the rocky tracks and slopes of Ningxia, Wang Zheng has caught the daily life of these pious desert peasants, never resigned to their fate, always working their earth in the expectation of ever more hypothetical rain. He has also been allowed into the great religious gatherings where cameras are usually banned. He has photographed the funeral of a regional head, the departure from the mosque after prayers, the start of a family meal . . .

He has managed to capture the soul of a region which would otherwise be a depressing statistic, condemned to disappearance. Wang Zheng calls himself a freelance photographer and now lives in Yinchuan, the capital of Ningxia.

The Land of Thirst

The lack of water makes itself felt through a myriad of details in the village of Zhangjiashu. The young imam of this mountain village of 1,008 souls, Hu Dengshuang, serves us tea made with melted snow, buried in winter in underground cisterns.

When such reserves are exhausted, the villagers go to the neighbouring commune to plead that a water truck be sent to them. Or they have to make do with the 'bitter water' which can be found an hour's walk away at the bottom of a ravine.

'With water, we could have a normal life here,' the imam says. Sometimes in order to conserve the precious liquid, he has to perform the ablutions before the five daily prayers using sand . . . He shows us. It's difficult to think of a better symbol of dryness than this ritual manner of representing an absence.

One evening, while we are debating things in a house in the village, a child comes in all excited. 'It's going to rain,' he announces. Everyone goes outside. The sky does, indeed, look heavy. A wind comes up. In the distance, lightning illuminates the horizon. We're all expecting rain, but after two or three drops, the sky clears. The storm passes us by without dropping its precious rain. Disappointed, the villagers go back into their houses.

When we were here in May 2001, the ground was dry and yellow, but the peasants continued to cultivate their smallholdings. They exhausted themselves pushing their ploughs over the arid ground, sometimes helped by a donkey or more rarely, an ox. A month later, when we came back, the hills were green. Had there been a miracle?

A peasant corrects us quickly. The wheat did indeed show itself, but because of the lack of water, it dried up instantly. Marking his words with a gesture, he picks up a stalk between his fingers. It crumbles. Only melons and beans planted beneath plastic awnings which gather the morning dew, can be harvested.

A year later, in July 2002, the exceptional rains which hit China gave this region its best harvest for twenty years. The dry slopes really did take on colour and a joyfulness which is somewhat false. Even with ideal climatic conditions, the level of underdevelopment here is such that the earth can't nourish all the inhabitants of Zhangjiashu.

If nature isn't of the most hospitable here, humans have done nothing to improve matters. The old people remember a time when this region, threatened by desertification, had plenty of trees. But they also sadly remember that these were cut down during the madness of the Great Leap Forward (1958–62), inaugurated by Mao Zedong, when every village was transformed into a great smelting oven in order to increase steel production. The peasants are still paying the price of that today.

A United Nations report in 1992 revealed that in certain districts of Ningxia, the population was between four and thirteen times greater than the earth could reasonably provide for. The report also noted that the availability of water in Ningxia was less than half the Chinese national average. There are great regional differences in the province, since the Huanghe, the Yellow River – one of the great waterways of China and, according to mythology, the cradle of the Chinese people – crosses it a little further north. But the Yellow River is also drying up. A great Pharaonic project devised by the Chinese government consists in diverting, ten years from now, one part of the flow of the Blue River, the Yangtse at the centre of the country, towards the Yellow River, in order to irrigate northern China. But this project would stop short of Ningxia.

Life here is so hard, everyone dreams of leaving, but there are few who can afford to do so. At the end of the 1990s, the Chinese government launched a programme to transfer populations some 150 kilometres north to the borders of the Yellow River. The plan was baptised '1-2-3-6', which translates from official Chinese jargon into 'one million people, two million mu, three billion yuan, six years'. You can see the canals and the pumping stations being built on the road to Yinchuan, only fifty kilometres away from Zhangjiashu.

But in four years only some 50,000 peasants have been able to leave their arid land for new, irrigated zones. The problem is that the peasants have to have personal means, which makes it impossible for most of them.

'People would love to be relocated elsewhere, but the costs are large and government help almost non-existent,' the imam tells us. He himself has chosen to stay with his flock and has convinced the local nurse to do the same. He had been tempted by the exodus. 'Without him, we'd have no access at all to basic care,' the imam underlines.

So the villagers of Zhangjiashu have no choice. Half of them meet government criteria for extreme poverty – all of them, if one uses the criteria of international organisations.[70] Some try as best they can to get something out of their arid land. Others try raising animals, perhaps a better alternative in this changing environment. All obey the government's order of the day which is to transform a

70 China crosses the poverty threshold at 635 yuan, or almost $80. The World Bank considers poverty to include anyone earning less than a dollar a day, or $365 a year, which is four times more than the sum Beijing uses. Thanks to these figures, the Chinese government could announce that it had substantially reduced poverty: only 26 million people out of a population of 1.3 billion. But if you use international criteria, the figures are quite different. According to the Bank for Asian Development (BAD), 230 million Chinese still live on less than a dollar a day, and 670 million on less than two dollars. (Figures based on the year 2000.)

part of their cultivated land into tree plantations in order to combat desertification. In exchange, they get subsidies in the form of sacks of grain.

Everywhere you go, you can see these fledgling trees, recently planted, which the Chinese hope will be ample enough to reverse decades of environmental neglect. On the national level, the authorities have launched a ten-year plan worth tens of billions of yuan and aimed at planting millions of trees.

The villagers of Zhangjiashu fully experience the marginalisation of the Chinese peasantry which represents two-thirds of the Chinese population of 1.3 billion. Starved and battered by excesses of the Maoist era largely forgotten today, then the first beneficiaries of the economic reforms introduced at the start of the 1980s, peasants now find themselves at the very bottom of the Chinese social ladder. The difference between their income and that of city dwellers continues to grow larger, while their political influence declines. This has become so dramatically the case that a well-known Beijing economist, Hu Angang, describes Chinese peasants as 'the largest single population in the world with no political representation'.[71]

Here is how Li Chanping, an old Communist village official whom we met in Beijing where he lived in exile after having written an open letter to the Prime Minister, describes the lot of the peasant: 'The peasant exodus is like a deluge, and the burden of the peasant as heavy as Mount Tai Shan. The peasants are riddled by a Himalaya of debt. Officials are akin to locusts, the system of responsibility is an instrument of torture and government measures mere fables in which lies become truths.'

The Chinese Prime Minister Zhu Rongji, addressed in this way, admitted publicly in the spring of 2002 that the lot of the peasants was his main 'headache'. All the reports show that the peasants

71 *Libération*, 5 February 2002.

will be the principal potential victims of China's entry into the World Trade Organization at the end of 2001. Chinese agriculture has remained archaic and will not be able to compete with the more cheaply produced foods from abroad. Ningxia will suffer more than the rest of China.

The government can see no other hope for Chinese agriculture than to back the rural exodus. A study carried out by a research centre directly tied to the Council of State, the highest level of Chinese government, estimated in May 2002 that approximately one-third of rural workers were not fully employed and that the surplus of rural workers numbered approximately 150 million. The study concluded: 'The transfer of the rural surplus to the non-rural sectors will be the only way to ensure a durable and healthy growth of the economy.'

One hundred and fifty million rural jobs to be moved into urban zones, 200 million according to a report by the OECD (Organization for Economic Cooperation and Development): the enormous challenge is on the scale of China itself. At Zhangjiashu, the Communist Party secretary exhorted inhabitants to go and find work elsewhere, even though the harvest of that year, 2002, was promising. 'There is no other solution,' he explained.

This 'floating population', as it is known in China, is made up of migrants of rural origin looking for either temporary or permanent work in the cities. Spotting the difference between comfortable citizens in the big cities and these immigrants from the interior, is easy. Their weathered skin and fearful eyes mark them out, as do their poor clothes and the fact that they're generally employed in tasks the city dwellers no longer want to do. They work on building sites, on rubbish dumps, in restaurants. Their fate is hardly enviable. They are despised, exploited, rejected . . .

Appeals regularly launched in the press by the authorities ask that the general population respect these men and women thrust on to the city streets by despair. Thus far, they have had little effect. In the meantime, peasants in search of work, like Ma Yan's father, are cast on the mercy of the new exploiting class in this reformed China. The Chinese Revolution, which owed everything to peasants, has turned its back on its origins.

The Islam of the Hui

Ningxia is a Muslim country. The identity of the region was built around the Islamic faith of the Hui people, distant descendants of the Arab or Persian merchants and emissaries who came to China on the Silk Route from the seventh century on. Today, they are close to the ethnic majority of Chinese, the Han, with whom they share a language – unlike the Uighur Muslims of Xinjiang province, culturally and ethnically anchored in Central Asia. Only their religious practice and certain of its outward signs, like the wearing of the distinctive white head-covering, distinguish them from the majority of Chinese.

The Constitution of the People's Republic, created in 1949, conferred 'nationality' on the Huis, according to a model imported from the Soviet Union by the remainder of the Communist world. 'Huis are Muslims, that is believers in a particular faith. But the authorities consider them as a nationality, a *minzu*, and to a certain extent they've interiorised this national designation. The tension between these two descriptions makes their identity problematic,' writes Elisabeth Alles, an expert on Chinese Islam, in her book *Musulmane de Chine*. Chinese Communist leaders, like those in the Soviet Union at the beginning of the twentieth century 'think it easier to deal with a national minority than with a community of faith'. The consequences of this approach are visible as far away as the former Yugoslavia, in the case of the Muslims of Bosnia-Herzegovina.

The clustering of the Hui in the arid mountains in the south of Ningxia is the result of religious persecution, war and rebellion in the eighteenth and nineteenth centuries. Two-thirds of the Hui in this region are in fact from Shaanxi, the neighbouring province, from where they fled during the repression by the Qing dynasty in the middle of the nineteenth century. The Hui were pushed back past the Chinese borders of that epoch. This makes it easier to see how these populations ended up in such inhospitable terrain.

Memories of that troubled time have remained alive among the eldest Hui. During a photo reportage, Wang Zheng met an old man who, on his way back from prayer time at the mosque, recalled the defeat of the Hui rebellion and his people's exodus as if it had happened yesterday. His ancestors had come from Yuqiao, in the south of the province of Shaanxi – which explains, Wang Zheng elucidates, why one finds a place called Yuqiao in the district of Xiji (one of the poles of the Xi Hai Gu triangle in the south of Ningxia). The old man's father had told him before he died: 'Remain serene. Pray to Allah calmly. Cultivate your land and live. That is what the Hui need to do.'

'We are a people shaped by history, not because the Communists decreed it,' Zhao Hui,[72] who is a Hui intellectual and professor at the University of Yinchuan, emphasises. She is the daughter of an old friend of Mao's, a member of a group of Muslim Communists. They formed an active battalion during the war against the Japanese and numbered an imam in their ranks. Her family line makes it possible for her to speak loudly and clearly in favour of the rights of the Hui, under-represented, as far as she is concerned, at the civil service level of the province in relation to their numbers.

Proud of her identity, she stresses that the Hui are united both by ties of blood and by religion. 'If a Han converts to Islam, he'll remain a Han. He won't have a blood link with the Hui.' She is concerned to accentuate this difference, to the point where she

72 Her given name is Hui, and though it looks like the same word as the ethnic grouping, it isn't because of the four tones of the Chinese language.

declares her sensitivity to the wearing of the veil by Pakistani women. She calls it 'very elegant' even though she comes to us bare-headed and dressed as a westerner.

But through this intransigent affirmation of identity – which she judges to be vital for a minority which can recognise itself by such symbols – is Zhao Hui not taking the risk of moving precisely in the direction of the fundamentalism she purports to condemn?

Islam has certainly been on the rise in Ningxia since the Cultural Revolution and its excesses came to an end. The Red Guard in their anti-religious fury destroyed most of the mosques, including the one in the regional capital of Yinchuan, which had been built in 1915. 'Worse still, Hui were forced to raise pigs,' Professor Zhao says indignantly.

Since then mosques have proliferated, alternating in style between the Chinese and the Middle Eastern and sometimes marrying the two in a surprising way. In the photo gallery of the big Nanguan mosque in Yinchuan, you can see pictures of soldiers helping workers, at the start of the 1980s, in the reconstruction of this building which has a Middle Eastern flavour. Superior officers of the People's Liberation Army at that time paid courtesy visits to imams.

Portraits of Mao Zedong, Deng Xiaoping and Jiang Zemin are also prominent in this religious building. This is both a sign of the prevailing calm between the state and Islam, and the latter's submission to official Communist power. 'Religious freedom is greater than it was ten years ago, but it has not yet reached the level which we, at heart, think necessary. There's still a way to go,' a Muslim dignitary told us.

Despite this, in the towns and villages of the province of Ningxia, the Communist Party, which is not known for its willingness to share power, has accommodated itself very well to the rise in Islamic influence. In one case, it was a Hui Party-Secretary himself who told us he went to Friday Prayers at the Mosque every week. 'I'm a Communist and therefore an atheist, but I need to be close to my people,' he said, without raising an eyebrow. Later, he confided that Islam played a central role in his life, that he respected its rules and transmitted them to his children, and tried, whenever possible, to avoid any contradictions between his faith and his Communist Party duties!

In the village of Zhangjiashu, which is 100 per cent Hui, the 34-year-old imam is certainly one of the figures of authority, alongside the traditional representatives of Communist power: the head of the village and the Party-Secretary. Like Wang Zheng, Imam Hu Dengshuang, the son of a former local official of the Party, has himself made the transition from Marx to Mohammed. This sometimes provokes some of the classic tensions between state and spiritual power, and in turn has an effect on the villagers. But the Party now allows such situations to develop, as long as there is no challenge to its legitimacy as the ultimate authority, both local and national.

We also met Hong Yang, the head of a Sufi brotherhood and visibly an important influence in the region. He holds the post of Vice-President in the local Parliament. As such, he's the very incarnation of a non-confrontational Islam which can live side by side with a central authority striving to stay in touch with its people.

This young Muslim dignitary, head of the Honghufuye brotherhood founded in the nineteenth century by his great-grandfather, studied Arabic in Beijing, then undertook many years of theological study at the Islamic University of Islamabad in Pakistan. There he was shoulder to shoulder with believers from everywhere in the Muslim world, including the Taliban. He even accompanied them to Afghanistan 'to see', but he judges their attitude towards women as excessive and also condemns the destruction by the Taliban of the giant Buddhist sculptures in Bamyan.

In 1999, with ten million yuan which had come as a gift from the Arab world, Hong Yang had a giant mausoleum built on the desert site where his ancestors, who had founded and run the Sufi brotherhood before him, are buried. The plans were drawn up by his own father. On his return from Mecca he devised a tomb which contains both Chinese and Islamic elements. In the desolate landscape where it stands, the mausoleum comes as a complete surprise. Every year, this holy site attracts hundreds of thousands of the faithful who come from Ningxia, Gansu or even from Xinjiang on a pilgrimage which is authorised by the government. All of this would have been impossible in China not so many years ago.

Hong Yang, who received us in great style in his large, modern, marble-floored house, underlined that his ancestors had 'always known how to maintain good relations with people in power', who-ever they were. 'Today, we get on well with the Communists.' This permits him to develop his influence by creating hundreds of mosques attached to his brotherhood. He has also established some thirty schools.

He is a critic of the local peasant mentality. 'They don't want to work hard. For a long time, they thought the Communist Party wouldn't let them die of hunger and they waited for aid.' During revolutionary days, this policy was called the 'iron rice bowl', which guaranteed a minimum of food whatever the work accomplished. This gradually fell away with the economic reforms undertaken by Deng Xiaoping during the 1980s.

In tune with the feeling of the times, Hong Yang's Friday sermons at the mosque stress enterprise. 'As a Muslim, you mustn't be con-tent with what you have. You must better your life and find a way of becoming more prosperous.' He encourages the young to go and work outside the region and to come back with investment funds. But, Hong Yang adds, the most important thing is education. 'The problem is the ignorance of the people.'

Ma Yan and her mother would concur. They live all the region's problems out on a daily basis.

The Plight of Education

The Chinese state no longer effectively responds to the thirst for education felt by the children of the Ningxia region who, far more than their parents, see it as their only hope of leaving misery behind. Education might theoretically be obligatory and universal up to the age of nine; Beijing may promise to eradicate illiteracy among fifteen to 24-year-olds by 2005; but the reality is a long way from such triumphalist proclamations. Education is getting worse. Children are excluded from school by their parents' poverty and there is no public safety net. Difficult enough in most Chinese rural regions, the situation is even worse in the west of the country and among the national minorities.

Ma Yaoguang, the district director of education, is responsible for fifty-six schools. Overcome by his lack of power, he confided to us, 'I have no means with which to help. I put forward a list of children in need, but if nothing comes back from the government, the children have to leave school. The drought has made everything worse. And for girls, it's even more difficult. All this is known in high places.'

Sometimes, he says, a little money comes through from Project Hope, a charitable organisation set up by the Chinese diaspora, but these funds are haphazard and resolve little. On top of that, at the beginning of 2002, a scandal erupted when it was found that the Project's funds had been gambled on the stock exchange.

The primary school in the village of Zhangjiashu receives one instructor's salary from the state: 800 yuan. The state also gives an indemnity of 50 yuan to the imam who teaches for free. That's it. Last year, the imam went to Beijing, with the help of a Chinese newspaper, to try and gather sponsorship money to support half of his pupils who were about to be taken out of school by families suffering from drought-induced poverty. He managed to find some private sponsors, still something new in China, and thus make up for the lack of state support.

This said, the Chinese Republic started off well enough. With only 20 per cent of children in school and 80 per cent of the population illiterate in 1949, the Communist regime inherited huge problems. Improvement came quickly and with consistency, and schools were built even in the most remote areas. But the Cultural Revolution of 1966–76 completely disorganised the educational system and it has never really recovered. With the economic reforms put in place from the end of the 1970s, schooling in the poorest communities – that is in the rural parts of China and most particularly in the national minority regions – started off by improving, only to deteriorate again through the 1990s. The Sinologist Claude Aubert talks of a 'sacrificed generation' in describing those children whose chances of education were utterly scuppered.

The educational sector, just like public health, has suffered doubly from the recent changes in Chinese society. On the one hand, it has been harmed by the mobilisation of resources for the profits of an urban minority and an elite which will ensure the rapid modernisation of the country. On the other, it has been badly affected by the decentralisation of resources and expenditure. This puts public finances and educational budgets into the hands of impoverished and often corrupt local authorities.

In May 2002, the government took on board the failure of this kind of decentralisation and put the finances and supervision of schools into the hands of larger district authorities. This is a modest step, though one which moves in the right direction, as long as it is backed up with effective, concrete action.

An OECD report on education in China, published in December 2001, revealed that the country only spent '3 per cent of its gross domestic product on all levels of education, which was about the same as in 1982. This needs to be compared with the 4.8 per cent spent by Brazil which is at a comparable level of development. The average level for the OECD is 6.1 per cent – ranging from 7.4 per cent in South Korea to 4.2 per cent in Luxembourg. In most of the countries of the OECD, between 1990 and 1996, spending on education rose at the same speed as national wealth. In China, the goal of the Ministry for Education is to move to 4 per cent of the gross domestic product, but this will still leave it behind many other countries.'[73]

The objective set in the mid-1990s had still not been met in 2002. The education budget rose less quickly than the defence budget which was already six times greater.

This situation is criticised even within China itself, especially when the underfunding of schools is seen to have tragic consequences. In March 2001, a violent explosion destroyed a primary school in the village of Fanglin in the province of Jiangxi in the south-west of China. Thirty-eight children and four teachers were killed. The official story that a madman had blown up the school in an attempt to commit suicide didn't stand up for long.

The parents' version was rather different. The children had been making fireworks in order to pay for the salaries of their teachers, when the terrible accident took place. Two weeks later, the Chinese Prime Minister, Zhu Rongji, who had defended the official version up until then, apologised in a live television broadcast and announced sanctions.

The accident drew attention to the fact that the situation in rural schools had become totally unacceptable. Teachers' salaries were regularly in arrears and the money nowhere to be had. A

73 OECD Report CCNM/CHINA/DEELSA, 2001.

member of parliament from Jiangxi even proposed a motion at the National Assembly demanding that the central government cover all educational expenses. But more than this will be necessary to reverse the situation.

China specialist Jasper Becker contends that 'the majority of rural teachers are peasants with no training whatsoever. 235 million Chinese schoolchildren are taught by 14 million teachers, of whom ten million need specialist training and three million have no qualifications whatsoever. Since 1991, up to 88 per cent of the education budget came from local government. The result was that teachers needed a second job, because schools were told to be self-sufficient. Villages had to pay for new schools themselves.'[74]

The plight of education rebounds on children and their parents, who are often taxed more heavily by local authorities. Alternatively, children are put to work to raise money, as in the tragic Jiangxi case which is far from unique. One thing is certain. Once poverty bites at parents' heels, in the way that it does in the drought-ridden villages of Ningxia, there is nothing to prevent the education system from disintegrating and an ever larger number of children from being excluded from it.

A case which appeared in the official Chinese press in April 2002 brought all this home once again to an indifferent urban public. A seven-year-old schoolboy was beaten to death by his impoverished peasant father in particularly horrific conditions because he wanted to go to school rather than work in the fields. The incident, reported by the *Law Daily* in Beijing, happened in Shandong. The father, infuriated by his son's refusal to work, beat him for seven hours at a stretch with a stick.

China has made enormous strides in taking its population out of misery. This success is what makes the regression now being

---

74 Jasper Becker, 'Hard lesson as education neglected', *South China Morning Post*, Hong Kong, 13 March 2001.

experienced by a part of its people even harder to bear. The children, who unlike their parents have had initial access to education, understand full well that this is the way out of the clutches of poverty. But no sooner are the doors opened than they close again.

At the same time, in the wealthier cities and even in part of the countryside, private education is springing up. This is endowed with all available technical resources, not to mention well-trained and well-paid teachers. From nursery to university, there are now 60,000 private education institutions in China, of which almost one hundred are universities. A recent law even permits these institutions to make a profit. Fees can be as high as several thousand, even tens of thousands, of yuan a year. These children of the new Chinese elite turn their backs on their peasant origins. They surf the net and will inevitably go to university in the United States. Meanwhile, children like Ma Yan struggle against hunger and exclusion. How much longer can China sustain these vast disparities?

Neither Ma Yan nor her mother exhibit any trace of rancour against the society which has forgotten them. Nor do they seem to resent their rich compatriots and a government which does so little for them. Even when Ma Yan recounts in her diary how she is refused a few vegetables by a comrade better off than she is, she doesn't harbour a grudge. She simply draws the conclusion that she is alone; she can only count on herself to make things better. In bad moments, this is a cause for despair; but it is also what gives her so much inner strength in her pursuit of her studies and a better life.

In this sense Ma Yan's diary is a lesson in courage for us all.